I Can Can Relishes, Salsa, Sauces & Chutney!!

How to make relishes, salsa, sauces, and chutney with quick, easy heirloom recipes from around the world so you can stock your pantry, give as gifts, or sell.

Jennifer Shambrook, Ph.D.

Author of Amazon Kindle Best Sellers

The Cornbread Bible: A Recipe Storybook

I Can Can Beef!!

I Can Can Chicken!!

Contributing Chefs and Co-Authors:

Tracy McLean, Jerusha Lee, Juleen Dickens, Patti Habbyshaw, Frank Wright, Terry Johnson, Rose Crawford and Cleo Russell

I CAN CAN!! Frugal Living Series, Volume 3

Proverbs 31 Press

All rights reserved by Jennifer Shambrook ©2013

Disclaimer

This is the part where I'm supposed to tell you that if you buy this book and start canning then do something silly like walk out your kitchen with the dish towel lying too close to the stove and burn your house down, I'm not going to buy you a new house, or even a new dish towel. Proceed at your own risk. I'm also supposed to tell you that this is my book, so don't go copying it and posting it on the internet or putting it in your book without asking me if it's okay first. If you do ask me, I'll probably be all flattered and flustered and everything and say that it's okay as long as you mention where you got it from, but please just ask first anyway. You can reach me through the I Can Can Relishes Facebook Page. I've got grandbabies so I'm on the Facebook way more than I ought to be. It's not hard at all to find me there! Stop by and say hey anytime.

Introduction

There are at least a dozen reasons why I have the relishes, salsa, sauces & chutneys you will learn to make in this book on my own pantry shelves. Home canned condiments:

1. Make plain meals seem special and festive.
2. Make great gifts.
3. Taste better than anything I can buy in the store.
4. Give me control over the food I feed my family.
5. Save me a fortune.
6. Allow me to preserve produce I lovingly grow in my own garden or buy locally.
7. Give me a great sense of self-satisfaction as I create my own pantry items.
8. Help me become more proficient in the domestic art of home canning.
9. Grant me the ability to tailor foods to suit the tastes of my family.
10. Help me inexpensively stock my pantry with delicious gourmet foods when produce is in season, at the peak of flavor, and at the best prices.
11. Give my friends a reason to bring bags of produce to me when their gardens or fruit trees over-produce and they don't want to see food go to waste.
12. Allow me to demonstrate my love for my friends and family by creating something special for them.

If any or some or all of those reasons resonate with you, keep reading. If you are new to canning, we will go step-by-step with every recipe and you will have a pantry lined with jars that look like beautiful culinary jewels! If you are a more experienced canner, dig in and pick up some more recipes for your pantry collection. If you can to sell, these are hot ticket items at farmer's markets and craft fairs.

Acknowledgements

Special thank yous go to Shannon Aldridge, Lin Ballew, my Facebook Prayer Posse who has encouraged me all the way, my family who has patiently waited for me to take a picture of something before we could eat on more than one occasion, and especially my extended family who have given me so many good folks to talk about.

Table of Contents

CANNING CAN BE EASY! 6

WATER BATH CANNING BASICS 9

   Selecting the Food 9

   Prepping the Food 9

   Work area 9

   Chopping 9

   Brining 10

   How about a nice hot bath? 10

   Canning with altitude! 12

   Tools of the trade: 12

RECIPES AND STORIES 14

   BLUE RIBBON SWEET PICKLE RELISH 16

      Blue Ribbon Sweet Pickle Relish Recipe 17

   BLUE RIBBON CHOW CHOW 19

      Blue Ribbon Chow Chow Recipe 20

   PEAR RELISH – TRACY MCLEAN'S FINEST 22

      Tracy's Pear Relish Recipe 23

   JERUSHY'S TOMATO RELISH 24

      Jerushy Recipe 25

      How to Easily Peel Tomatoes 26

   QUEENSLAND CORN, TOMATO & PINEAPPLE RELISH 27

      Queensland Relish Recipe 29

   KENTUCKY KETCHUP 30

      Kentucky Ketchup Recipe 31

   SWEET PEPPER RELISH 32

      Sweet Pepper Relish Recipe 32

   CAPONATA – A MEDITERRANEAN EGGPLANT RELISH 33

- *Caponata Recipe* *34*
- BRANSTON PICKLE 35
  - *Shamston Pickle Recipe* *37*
- SALSA ROJA – AN EASY AND SIMPLE GARDEN SALSA 39
  - *Salsa Roja Recipe* *41*
  - *Uncle Terry's Mexican Meatloaf Recipe* *42*
- SALSA VERDE SOUTHERN STYLE – MADE WITH GREEN TOMATOES 43
  - *Salsa Verde Southern Style Recipe* *44*
- HUNGARIAN PEPPER MUSTARD SAUCE 45
  - *Hungarian Pepper Mustard Sauce Recipe* *46*
- AUSTRALIAN RED ONION RELISH 47
  - *Red Onion Relish Recipe* *48*
- HOME CANNED BARBECUE SAUCE 49
  - *Barbecue Sauce Recipe* *50*
- CHUTNEY: A SHAMBROOK FAMILY FAVE 51
  - *Chutney Recipe* *52*
  - *Cran-Apple Jelly from peelings and cores* *53*
- CRANBERRY-ORANGE RELISH WITH TRIPLE SEC – AN EVERYDAY HOLIDAY 54
  - *Cranberry-Orange Relish with Triple Sec Recipe* *55*
- GERMAN RED CABBAGE – IT WAS FASCINATION 56
  - *German Red Cabbage Recipe* *57*
- ASIAN PLUM SAUCE FOR ZHANG XIAO YUN JOHNSON 59
  - *Asian Plum Sauce Recipe* *60*
- ROBERT'S HOT PEPPER SAUCE (FROM THE CORNBREAD BIBLE: A RECIPE STORYBOOK) 61
  - *Robert's Hot Pepper Sauce Recipe* *61*
- FIESTA SALAD FROM I CAN CAN BEEF 62
- I CAN CAN!! FRUGAL LIVING SERIES 63
  - *Frugal Living Series works in progress* *63*
- ABOUT THE AUTHOR 64

Canning Can Be Easy!

Imagine having a pantry stocked full of fabulous relishes, delicious sauces, jars of salsa, and exotic chutney. Those jars are on hand when you want to give a special hostess gift to a friend. Those jars are there to add something special to your favorite recipes. Those jars are on hand to make a simple meal seem like a holiday.

Speaking of holidays, just imagine giving holiday baskets with home canned treats to your friends and family. You may even be thinking of canning some special relishes or sauces to earn a little extra income or for a fund-raiser.

With your home canned relishes, salsa, sauces and chutneys, you know you have the finest, hand-picked ingredients with no chemical preservatives. You chose the plums that are in your plum sauce. And your plum sauce actually has little bits of plums that you can see. Your salsa is as hot or mild as you like. You control the sodium, you control the amount of garlic, you control the amount of sugar. You have a supply of food on hand to serve to your family or give away or sell that is delicious and prepared exactly to your own flavor specifications.

What if I don't know anything about canning?

That is not a problem because it is easy to do as long as you have someone to show you how to do it. That is why I am writing this book. I want my children, grandchildren, and great-great-great grandchildren to know these family recipes and the stories that go along with them. Canning was once a common practice that everyone knew how to do. Unfortunately, that is no longer the case. Water bath canning is not hard at all. I learned to can when I was a just a girl. I want to teach it to you. It's even easier now than when I learned, because we have the food processor and slow-cooker as well as fruits and vegetables available to us year round.

Are you required to use a food processor to create the recipes in this book? Heavens, no! There are some things I prefer to chop by hand, just because it is prettier. But if you own one or can borrow one for the weekend, it will make the time requirements considerably less on some of the recipes.

What will I learn in this book?

You will learn to can relishes, salsa, sauces and chutney from around the world. I spent my childhood in the foothills of Alabama where I learned to can and live a frugal, sustainable lifestyle. I spent my adult life seeing as much of the world as I could and eating as much good food as I could. There are recipes in this book from all over the world. You will find Mediterranean, Asian, German, Indian, Australian, British, Hungarian, All American, and of course, good ol' Southern recipes.

You will learn step-by-step how to make the very same recipes I make that have been winning blue ribbons at food competitions for over 20 years. I'm not holding back any secrets. I want your recipe to be as wonderful as mine. Before you know it, your pantry will be full of a variety of wonderful things to make your meals even better. I have included every step. And, if you have a question, you can even get in touch with me through the I Can Can Relishes, Salsa, Sauces and Chutney Facebook page.

Even if you don't have a question, I hope you'll stop by and say hello or include more recipes that you find and think folks might enjoy trying.

Why should I can my own?

Three words will answer that question: flavor, quality, and control. Factory processed foods just do not have the flavor of home-canned foods. Food canned in factories has to suit the "general" palate. Food canned in your kitchen has to suit YOUR palate. Which do *you* think will be more sensitive to exactly the way you want something to taste?

Quality is a huge issue with me. As you follow these recipes, you won't be adding artificial flavors or fillers or extenders. Your recipe will include fresh farm products right out of your own garden, or hand selected by you at your favorite grocer or farm stand.

Controlling of the level of sugar, or type of sugar, or amount of sodium or garlic or hot chili peppers enables you to tailor the food your family eats to exactly what you want or need. There is also a deep sense of satisfaction in creating your own foods for your pantry. Seeing all of those jars lined up on your shelves is comforting to your heart.

How is this book arranged?

We will start with a little overview of the water bath canning process and the tools you will use. Then we will move on to the recipes and stories. This is not just a cookbook, it is a recipe storybook. If you have read the previous books in the Frugal Living Series (I Can Can Beef and I Can Can Chicken) they consist of the canning process, then recipes for using the canned meats. In this book, there are individual canning recipes from around the world, which includes serving suggestions.

The recipes in this book are the recipes I make for my own pantry shelves. They are delicious. As we say in Alabama: No brag, just fact. If they weren't so incomparably scrumptious, I promise, I wouldn't go to the trouble of making them.

Each recipe was inspired by someone that I love and want to introduce you to. I've included little stories that I want to preserve about people that I love. Some of the folks in these stories aren't physically here anymore, but as I tell the story or re-read the story, it's like having a little hug and chuckle with them. Also, I get to introduce my old friends to you, my new friend. I hope you will enjoy reading the stories. I also hope that reading these few little paragraphs about my loved ones will remind you of some of your own stories about the important people in your life and perhaps inspire you to tell them or write them down for your family and friends.

If you are only interested in the recipes and want to skip the stories, don't worry, I won't be offended. I've designed the Table of Contents so you can easily skip the stories. Just don't tell me and I'll never know!

So what makes me the big hotshot expert on canning?

Well, I guess over fifty years of experience, if you count helping shell peas and stringing beans on Granny Tom's porch before I was ten gives me some credibility. I also have drawers full of blue ribbons from multiple fairs. (That's drawers as in dresser drawers, not undergarments!)

Everyone is good at a thing or two. My thing or two happens to be teaching and canning, so writing and sharing this information with you helps me to use the talents I have been given. Doing so genuinely brings joy to my heart. I really want to pass this domestic art along to others. Preserving preserving, you might say. So please read on and get ready to stock your pantry with relishes, salsa, sauces and chutney from around the world!

Water Bath Canning Basics

I will give you step-by-step instructions for each of the recipes, but it is a good idea to just read over these basics to familiarize yourself with the water bath canning process. Also, when you are going to make a recipe, it is a good idea to read over the recipe, make your grocery list, assemble your ingredients, then read over the recipe one more time before you start. It will make things go much smoother.

Selecting the Food

Choose the best quality food you can afford to buy. Look over your produce. Try to get the freshest possible ingredients. I like to either grow my own or buy locally, if possible. If there are blemishes, you can always just cut them out. I will take home grown or local with a blemish over perfect weeks-old imports. Be a little picky here. Just keep in mind, you are preparing this food to eat for a year, or give to someone dear, so take the time to choose the prettiest and freshest fruits and vegetables you can find.

Prepping the Food

It is always a good practice to assemble everything you are going to need and measure out your ingredients before you start cooking. It makes the cooking so much easier if everything is pre-measured beforehand. The fancy chefs call it *mise en place* which means, everything is in place. I don't want to be looking for a measuring spoon, or an ingredient, or even measuring, when it is time to put the recipe together. I want to prep, assemble, cook, process, and then listen to those jar lids pop like a little round of canning jar salutes.

Work area

Your work area needs to be absolutely spotless as you prepare any canned foods. You don't want all of your hard work to go for naught because a bacteria invaded through uncleanliness. Have your equipment ready (there is a list of equipment needed below) and make sure it is all clean. You will need to have paper towels ready to wipe up spills, or wipe rims. Your kitchen is your food preservation laboratory while you are involved in the canning process.

If you have long hair, or hair that hangs into your face, it's a good idea to tie or pin it back, so you won't be tempted to touch your hair while you are involved in the canning process. Heaven forbid if a hair should escape and you give someone a jar of hairy relish!

You may be standing for a while in the same place. If you have hard tile floors, you may want to put a rug under where you will stand and wear comfortable shoes.

One more thing, remember ever being told "You should have done that before we left the house?" Well, if you do, just think about it and see if there is one more thing you need to do before you get started.

Chopping

I don't think sharp knives are as dangerous as dull ones. Sharpen all of your knives before you start chopping. Even if you are using a food processor, you will have to rough chop to get things to the right size to fit in the food processor. If a knife is sharp, you don't have to apply as much pressure, therefore you have more control with the blade.

I sharpen my knives as I am assembling my tools. I wash all of my fruit or vegetables, then chop everything at one time without having to stop and wash again. If you have help in the kitchen, you could have someone else washing while you are chopping and using the food processor, but if you are a one person kitchen crew, I think it is easier to wash everything, peel everything, rough chop, then process everything.

Brining

Some of the recipes call for brining overnight. This is a process where the vegetable is mixed with salt and left overnight so that the salt can draw the moisture from the vegetables. Do not skip this step, it really does make a difference in your end product. Some vegetables have a lot of water in them and if this step is omitted, you will end up with a watery product with a less concentrated flavor. Brining intensifies the flavors as well as reducing the water content of the end product.

When you brine, you will need a non-reactive vessel of some kind. I have two that I routinely use. One is an old crockery fermenter that my Aunt Brenda gave me. She and Uncle Lloyd used it to make kraut. Before she gave me that, I used a food grade 5 gallon bucket along with the lid from one of my water bath canners. You could also use a plastic dish pan. Just make sure it is clean and not something that the salt will "react" with, like aluminum.

How about a nice hot bath?

To do boiling water bath canning, you are going to need a large pot… a VERY large pot. The size of the pot will need to be big enough to hold all of your canning jars with an inch or two of water on top of them. That water is intended to be at a rolling boil, so the sides of the pot are going to need to be tall enough to not splash boiling water over the sides when it is boiling.

I actually have four pots that I use for boiling water bath canning. They are different sizes and I choose the pot that will work best with the size jars I am using. I have to use my monster-sized one if I am canning quarts or a huge batch of pints. I use a smaller one for smaller batches or half-pint jars. It takes more time to heat more water, so I try to use a smaller water bath canner if I can get away with it and get all my jars in.

If you don't have one or you are just getting started, they are very reasonably priced. You can certainly manage with just one, but you should start with a really large one that will accommodate any size jar. You may think you would never can anything in a quart jar, but I promise, once you get started canning, and taste your own wonderful home-canned foods, you will be hooked. You'll find yourself canning all kinds of things.

To use the water bath canner, you will heat your water to a boil while you are preparing your food to go into the sterilized jars. Remember that your jars will displace a good bit of the water, so allow for that when you are determining how much water to add. When you lower your jars into the boiling water, it will reduce the temperature of the water to below boiling. Keep your stove turned to high and bring the water back to a rolling boil before you start counting your processing time.

I let my water bath canner do double duty to sterilize my jars. I start with clean jars, then put them in the water bath canner as the water is heating. The water heats to boiling and sterilizes the clean jars as it boils. I remove the jars from the water bath canner using the jar lifter and fill the hot jars with the hot relish, salsa, sauce or chutney. I remove some of the boiling water from the water bath with a small saucepan and put my jar lids in there to soften the compound. The lids do not need to boil, but the compound needs to soften in order to get a good seal.

I can all throughout the year producing several hundred of jars of food for my pantry. Seal failure is very rare. I may have one jar out of a hundred that will not get a good seal. To get a good seal there are three main things you need to remember:

1. Place the lid in boiling hot water, as described above, to soften the compound on the lids.
2. Wipe the rim of the jar with a moistened paper towel. Fold and refold the paper towel so that you are using a clean side with every jar. The rim of the jar should be completely clean and free of food or juice.
3. Hand tighten the rings to snug, but not need-a-wrench-to-remove tight.

Another good thing to remember: always use a timer. It is too easy to get distracted, or miscalculate, and too important that the time be followed accurately, to use a clock or guesstimate if it's been ten minutes. Do not start the timer as soon as you put the jars into the water. The jars, though very hot, will be lower than the boiling point. **Allow the water to return to a rolling boil, then start your timer and always go for the full time.**

Keep safety in mind when working with boiling water. When you handle the jars, use a canning jar lifter. Be very careful lifting the jars and placing them into the boiling water bath. You don't want to splash boiling water on yourself or anyone else in the kitchen. Also, the jars are fragile, so you want to be careful with them for that reason as well. You will also use your canning jar lifter to bring the jars out of the water.

The jars will need to cool in a place that does not have a draft. They should be placed on a surface that is protected, as the jars are very hot. Also remember, a hot jar placed on a cold surface is very likely to break. Cover your countertop or table with several thicknesses of toweling, or use a wooden cutting board or cooling racks for your jars to sit on while they cool.

After the jars cool, you will hear the lids POP as the seals engage. It is one of my favorite sounds! Once the jars have cooled, check your jars to ensure that all jars have sealed. When you press down on the center of the jar, they should not "give" but be a bit concave and firm. If a jar did not seal, you can re-process, or just put the jar in the refrigerator and use it within a week.

Canning with altitude!

All of the recipes in this book show the processing times for sea level up to 1,000 feet above sea level. If you live at a higher altitude, you probably already know you are special and have to make special adjustments to make recipes do what they are supposed to do. Use this chart to make adjustments to the recipes for your altitude.

Altitude (Feet)	Added Processing Time
1,001 – 3,000	+ 5 minutes
3,001 – 6,000	+10 minutes
6,001 – 8,000	+15 minutes
8,001 – 10,000	+20 minutes

Tools of the trade:

So, what are you going to need? We have already talked about the need for a water bath canner and sharp knives. You will also need measuring cups and spoons. Large bowl-sized measuring cups come in really handy when you need large quantities of an ingredient.

If you have a food processor, you will save yourself a lot of chopping time. There will be times, though, that you are going to want to chop by hand to get a prettier result. In that case, you will want sharp knives handy. My Granny used a mandolin. This scary looking little instrument looks like something that would give Marie Antoinette flashbacks. It is incredibly sharp, but also incredibly effective in quickly slicing or shredding fruits and vegetables. But please be careful! I use and recommend the Progressive Folding Mandolin which you kind find on Amazon for around $20 at the time of this writing.

You will likely need several large bowls and some smaller cups or bowls to hold your pre-measured ingredients as you prepare to can and get *mise en place*. The larger bowls may also hold your chopped or washed ingredients as you get those together. As mentioned above, some of the recipes will require a very large vessel to hold vegetables for brining overnight. After brining, you will need to drain and for that you will need a very large colander.

Of course, you will need canning jars. While I have seen people can in "leftover" jars from the store, reusing the lids, I don't do it and I don't recommend it. The FDA recommends buying jars and lids that are especially manufactured for home canning. You can find them at Big Lots, Fred's, Wal-Mart, and some grocery stores. In the recipes, I have recommended canning jar sizes and estimated yields so that you will know how many jars and lids to prepare.

To fill your jars, you will need a canning funnel and either a ladle or canning scoop. I recommend using a canning scoop because it is designed to scrape the edges of the pot to get the last of your precious relish or chutney from the pot. It also holds more than a common ladle and the handle design makes it easier to fill the jars. If you don't have a set of canning instruments, you can get them from Amazon or any of the stores mentioned above that sell jars.

You will need a jar lifter to place the jars in the boiling water and safely lift them back out. A canning jar lid magnet, canning jar lids, and rings are also necessities. In order for the jars to seal, the lids have a waxy compound on them that has to be heated prior to the sealing process. They don't have to be boiled, but they should be heated almost to the boiling point. The lid magnet will help you lift the flat lids out of the hot water and place them on the jars.

After you have finished processing your jars, they need to sit on a surface covered with folded towels, a wooden chopping board, or wire cooling racks. (I know I'm repeating myself, but this is important!)

I recently treated myself and upgraded to the Progressive brand canning tools. I still have my old Ball set of tools that I used for decades. You may find it handy to keep all of your small canning tools in a basket or re-usable cloth shopping bag with your spare lids and rings. When you get ready to can, just grab that basket or bag and you will have everything together in one place ready for your next canning adventure. I started doing that, and bought the spare upgrade set that I now most frequently use, after my canning funnel was misplaced and I spent 45 minutes tearing up my kitchen and laundry room looking for it. Save yourself that little frustration and learn from my mistakes, dear readers!

Recipes and Stories

I try to write the I Can Can books imagining that you are in my kitchen, helping me as I prepare each of these recipes. Sometimes, the chopping takes a bit of time, so I cannot stop myself from trying to keep you entertained (and chopping), by telling you a story about the recipe, or the person that developed the recipe. I cook as an expression of love, so it is only natural for me to tell you about the people I love as I share these recipes with you.

With my other cookbooks, many readers have said how much they love the stories. There are always one or two who say they didn't really want to read the stories, they just wanted the recipes. I am also aware that my story-loving readers might want to read through the book once, then go back to the recipes that they are eager to take for a test drive and might not want to read the story again. For those reasons, I have tried to organize this section so that it is clear where the story stops and the recipe and recipe notes start.

The recipes here are representative of what you will find in my own pantry. I have loosely arranged these recipes starting with my very favorite store-bought-can't-touch-it recipe, Blue Ribbon Sweet Pickle Relish. The pickle relish is followed by a similar recipe called chow chow. If you haven't heard of it before, chow chow is a Southern staple relish that is eaten with vegetables. After chow chow is a Leeds-local recipe that you can't even buy in the store called Jerushy. This is also made to be served with vegetables. Jerushy is a recipe that has been in my family for over one hundred years.

I move from relishes to be served with vegetables to recipes served as a snack, like salsa and caponata. After that we go to recipes to be served with meats like Juleen's Red Onion Relish and Asian Plum Sauce. That's how I group them in my pantry, so it is just pure Jennifer-logic.

If it seems like I have a gigantic family with hundreds of relatives, it's because I do. My grandmother, Hazel Carlisle had five sisters and two brothers. My grandfather, Ruby Ernest Johnson had five brothers. The Carlisle girls had a Cherokee mother and the Johnson boys had a Creek mother. Two of the Carlisle girls, Hazel and Ellen, married two of the Johnson brothers, Ernest and Wesley. Papa Johnson, gave each of the newlywed couples forty acres of land from his farm. During the depression years, they each had eight kids, worked the land, supplemented that by working in the coal mines, and did what they could to help each other make ends meet. Both families had five boys and one girl live to adulthood, and both families had to bear the heart-wrenching grief of having two children to die in childhood. The families have always been loving and close. It isn't surprising that all the double first cousins looked alike and acted like brothers and sisters.

I call all of Daddy's double first cousins and their spouses Aunt and Uncle, ma'am and sir. When you combine the double first cousins with Daddy's siblings and their spouses, I have twenty-two aunts and uncles. All of them now have kids, grandkids, and great-grandkids. I also had twenty-two great-aunts and uncles... and this is just on my Daddy's side.

I have five more aunts and uncles through Mama. She also had 35 first cousins. Both families were very close. So yes, it seems like I have hundreds of relatives because I actually do. The truly miraculous blessing of this is that we all love each other and truly enjoy spending time together. When we are together, we like to eat and tell stories about our kinfolk and days gone by. This recipe storybook is just one of those visits in written form.

Now that you have had to wade through all of that, it's time for me to introduce you to some foods and folks that I love.

Pictured below are Asian Ginger Plum Sauce, Caponata, and Hungarian Pepper Mustard.

Blue Ribbon Sweet Pickle Relish

"These are the best devilled eggs I've ever tasted!" is a phrase I hear often and a phrase I absolutely love to hear. Of course, that phrase is usually followed with "what is your secret?" Well, folks, that's what I am about to share with you.

This is where it all started. My canning adventures were sealed as a permanent life-time endeavor the first time I made sweet pickle relish. It was like magic in a jar. There are three very simple and inexpensive things I love to eat: hotdogs, devilled eggs, and tuna salad. But there is one problem, they all require pickle relish to qualify as properly prepared and "store bought" pickle relish is only a shadow of what pickle relish should be.

The pickle relish you purchase in the store does not have the distinct flavors of the vegetables that are in the relish. It is a very questionable shade of green, compliments of dyes, with only a few flecks of red. The flavors of the spices are essentially non-existent. The texture is mushy. Bottom line: It isn't pretty enough, tasty enough, or firm enough to satisfy my hotdog, devilled egg or tuna salad requirements.

My canning escapades have had many productivity peaks and valleys. In some years I canned everything I could get my hands on. In other years, especially when I was working and going to school, I only canned a few things. In some years, I canned one or two things. If I only canned one thing, it was sweet pickle relish. If I only canned two things, it was sweet pickle relish and the recipe you'll see later called Jerushy.

Over the years, I have perfected this recipe to my own tastes. I love for my pickle relish to look like a colorful jar of gemstones. A little over twenty years ago, an elderly girlfriend of my Mammaw, Mrs. Clovestine Alexander, decided that she would take a jar of my pickle relish and enter it into the Alabama State Fair. She entered it and it won a ribbon. She did that for two years. Encouraged by her example, the third year, I entered it myself. It won best of show and my prize was a Ball Blue Book Canning Guide. Since then, my pickle relish has won a drawer full of ribbons in fairs in Alabama, South Carolina, and Tennessee.

The ribbons are fun, but jars of relish in my pantry are essential. The feeling of self satisfaction when I load up hotdogs with homemade relish and homemade sauerkraut, or delicious tuna salad stuffed tomatoes for my family far outweighs the happiness of winning a ribbon. Being asked the question, "What is your secret with these devilled eggs?" makes me smile my biggest smile. Of course, the answer always is: "I can my own relish."

Every now and then, someone will say, "Will you teach me how to make it?" I have always said that I would, so now, after all these years, I am going to keep that promise. I'm telling all of my secrets... at least all of my secrets about this recipe! You will be surprised to find that although the recipe is a little time consuming, it is very easy. Don't be surprised if you suddenly become the one that is always expected to bring devilled eggs to the potluck or picnic! Mammaw had hens, so she always brought devilled eggs to our gatherings. Now I like to bring them as a tribute to her.

Blue Ribbon Sweet Pickle Relish Recipe

You can use your food processor to cut the vegetables, but it won't be quite as pretty if you do. If I am in a hurry and don't have the time to chop the vegetables by hand, I will use my food processor. The taste is delicious either way, but if you want the absolutely most beautiful results, cut all of the vegetables being chopped into small quarter inch pieces by hand.

You need to use pickling cucumbers in this recipe. Salad cucumbers have too much water in them. If you don't know the difference, ask your grocer, or better yet, grow your own! Cucumbers grow on a vine and are very prolific! We grow picklers and use them both for canning relish and eating in salads, thinly sliced on tuna salad sandwiches, or just on their own!

Ingredients

- 5 cups chopped pickling cucumbers
- 3 cups chopped onions
- 1 cup chopped sweet green bell pepper
- 1 cup chopped sweet red bell pepper
- 1 cup chopped sweet yellow bell pepper
- 1 cup finely chopped carrot
- 1/4 cup salt
- 3 1/2 cups sugar
- 2 cups apple cider vinegar
- 1 1/2 Tablespoon mustard seed
- 1 1/2 Tablespoon celery seed
- 2 teaspoons (about 2 cloves) very finely chopped garlic

Instructions

1. Chop all of your vegetables and put them in a large container.
2. Sprinkle with salt and thoroughly mix through the vegetables.
3. Add enough cold water to just cover salted vegetables.
4. Allow to brine for 2-3 hours. (Go watch a movie, you deserve it after all that chopping.)
5. Pour vegetables into a large colander and allow to drain for 30 minutes to one hour as you prepare jars, set up your water bath canner, prepare your vinegar, and get ready to can.
6. Fill your water bath canner half full with water and begin to heat to boiling.
7. Place 6-7 clean pint jars in the water bath canner and then heat to boiling.
8. After the water begins to boil, place jar lids in a small sauce pan and pour boiling water over lids to soften sealing compound.
9. In another pot large enough to hold vinegar mixture and the vegetables, combine vinegar, sugar, garlic and spices. Bring to a boil while stirring occasionally to dissolve sugar.
10. Press two thicknesses of paper towels into vegetables to help squeeze out all of the excess water.
11. Put vegetables into boiling vinegar mixture.

12. Return to a boil while stirring.
13. Reduce heat and simmer for 10 minutes.
14. Remove jars from water bath canner using the jar lifter.
15. Fill jars using canning scoop and canning funnel leaving 1/4 inch head space.
16. Wipe jar rim with dampened paper towel.
17. Fit with lids and rings. Adjust rings to finger tight using kitchen towel and oven mit to protect yourself from hot jars.
18. Return to boiling hot water bath.
19. Repeat until all jars are filled.
20. Bring to boil and process 10 minutes.
21. Remove jars from hot water bath and place on cooling racks or several thicknesses of folded towels.

Yield: 6-7 pints.

To make devilled eggs, just hard boil your eggs, peel, cut in half and remove the yolks. Crumble the cooked yolks into a small bowl, add a little pickle relish and a little mayonnaise then mix together. Salt and pepper to taste. Fill the cooked egg whites with egg yolk mixture. Sprinkle with paprika and garnish with olive slices or tiny parsley sprigs.

To make tuna salad, drain tuna and place in a small bowl. Add a stalk chopped celery, a chopped boiled egg, a little mayo, some pickle relish then stir together. Serve on sandwiches, on top of a tossed salad, or on tomato wedge roses. Pickle relish is also good in potato salad, macaroni salad, or any other way you normally like to eat pickle relish. Below is relish made last year with cukes from Candy Cannon.

Blue Ribbon Chow Chow

Chow Chow is a staple in many southern pantries. It is eaten as a condiment with field peas or just to add an interesting flavor combination to any plate of food. I like it best with field peas, black eyed peas, crowder peas or lady peas. Of course, the chow chow adorned peas would be served with cornbread. With that, and perhaps a sliced tomato and a green onion, that's about all I'm going to need for dinner and perfect contentment.

I will say, however, I have been able to get through much of my life without having to manufacture my own chow chow. With most canners, there is a bit of an unofficial coop that seems to form. This is how it often goes… "I made a big batch of this, and you made a big batch of that, so let's do a little swapping." Another way I would get my chow chow groove on would be to just see an open jar sitting beside the peas at a potluck. Since I usually have Jerushy for peas at my house, I would just eat chow chow when I was somewhere that someone else had it on the table, or someone would give me a jar.

My chow chow behavior had to change this year. My very beloved cousin, Donna Jean Johnson Lauderdale, sent me a Facebook message to ask me if I had a good chow chow recipe. I told her that I didn't have one, but I could use one if she had it. She said she didn't have a good recipe, but needed one because she was really craving some chow chow. I love my cousin Donna Jean, so I made it my business to find or develop a suitable recipe. Something had to be done about those chow chow cravings!

I had already decided I was going to write this book this summer, and the book wouldn't be complete if it didn't have a good chow chow recipe in it. Her request was all the prompting I needed to find a recipe. I started asking around. Everyone that I used to know who made chow chow has already gone on to their heavenly rewards. All of my chow-chow experts: Aunt Joyce, her Mama, Mrs. Brock, up in Cullman, Alabama, some of the ladies at Bold Springs Church, they are all gone. Not only were they gone, so were their chow chow recipes, apparently. No one could even locate a recipe. And as I asked, more people were after me to come up with a good one and give it to them when I did!

I was afraid, at that point, that if I didn't figure out a way to reproduce that chow chow goodness, this wonderful jar of sweet and tart flavors might fade off into the sunset. My next step was to start sifting through recipes from my cookbook collection and the internet. Based on the way I remembered it tasting, I settled on four recipes that I thought I could combine and tweak and add a little cinnamon to to get it just right. Happily, the experiment was a success. Just wait until you hear what happened!

Chow chow construction is very similar to making sweet pickle relish, so I felt pretty confident. With a little fine tuning, it turned out just the way I remembered. I knew how I wanted it to taste and look. I don't know if it was beginner's luck or all those years chopping vegetables for sweet pickle relish or a divine intervention from one of those kind ladies that used to bless the church suppers with chow chow. As I was cooking, the house filled with the wonderful old time smell of chow-chow. I liked it so much I even entered it into the Delta Fair this year. I was so tickled when my sweet pickle relish came in second place with a red ribbon and the chow chow won the blue ribbon for first prize!

I'm offering the recipe here for you, but the first copy went to my inspiration and dear cousin, Donna Jean.

Blue Ribbon Chow Chow Recipe

This can be made using a mandolin or knife to finely shred the cabbage and chop the vegetables by hand. Because it makes such a big batch and takes so long, you may want to purchase or borrow a food processor if you don't have one. They can really save you a lot of time.

The recipe is chopped one day and canned the next, so it is great for a weekend project.

I use a food grade five gallon bucket with the lid for my water bath canner on top for my overnight brine.

If your canner won't hold 10-12 pint jars at once, you can divide this into two batches. Just re-heat the chow chow and repeat steps 7 and 8 then 13 through 20.

Ingredients

- 4 cups chopped cabbage (one small to medium head)
- 4 cups chopped onions
- 4 cups chopped green tomatoes
- 4 cups chopped sweet bell peppers in various colors (red, green, yellow)
- 4 cups chopped or shredded carrots
- 1/2 cup kosher or canning salt
- 4 cups granulated sugar
- 2 cups brown sugar, packed firm
- 2 Tablespoons mustard seed
- 2 Tablespoons celery seed
- 1 1/2 teaspoons turmeric
- 1 teaspoons cinnamon
- 1/2 teaspoon ginger
- 4 cups distilled white vinegar
- 1 cup water

Instructions

1. Using a food processor, chop the vegetables finely and place in a large, non-reactive container (plastic, glass, or porcelain).
2. Cover with salt and mix together well.
3. Cover container and let sit overnight to brine.
4. Pour vegetables into a large colander and lightly rinse with cold water
5. Allow to drain while preparing water bath canner, jars and vinegar solution.
6. Fill your water bath canner to half full with water and begin to heat to boiling.
7. Place 10-12 clean pint jars in the water bath canner to heat to boiling.
8. After the water begins to boil, place jar lids in a small sauce pan and pour boiling water over lids to soften sealing compound.

9. In another pot large enough to hold vinegar solution and the vegetables, combine the remaining ingredients. Bring to a boil while stirring occasionally to dissolve sugar.
10. Carefully add the vegetables to the vinegar solution being careful not to splash the hot vinegar on yourself.
11. Stir all ingredients together and bring to a boil.
12. Allow to simmer for five minutes and turn off heat.
13. Remove jars from water bath canner using the jar lifter.
14. Fill jars using canning scoop and canning funnel leaving 1/4 inch head space.
15. Wipe jar rim with dampened paper towel.
16. Fit with lids and rings. Adjust rings to finger tight using kitchen towel and oven mit to protect yourself from hot jars.
17. Return to boiling hot water bath.
18. Repeat until all jars are filled.
19. Bring to boil and process 10 minutes.
20. Remove jars from hot water bath and place on cooling racks or several thicknesses of folded towels.

Yield: 8-9 pints

Pear Relish – Tracy McLean's Finest

Tracy McLean is a much sought after chef in her part of the state of Georgia. She caters events and can make even the simplest fare seem fancy and special. She's got that special knack that just seems to make everything she cooks look and taste special. She has further developed her natural talents by formally training as a chef.

Tracy is generous with her talents and spends a lot of time these days in the kitchen of her hundred-plus year old Victorian home. When she is not in the kitchen, you may find her in her garden. She offers her organically grown vegetables and home-canned foods at local farmers' markets and craft events in and around her home town of Royston. She is a co-author of The Cornbread Bible, so you will see those at her Farmer's Market stand as well, as you can see shown below.

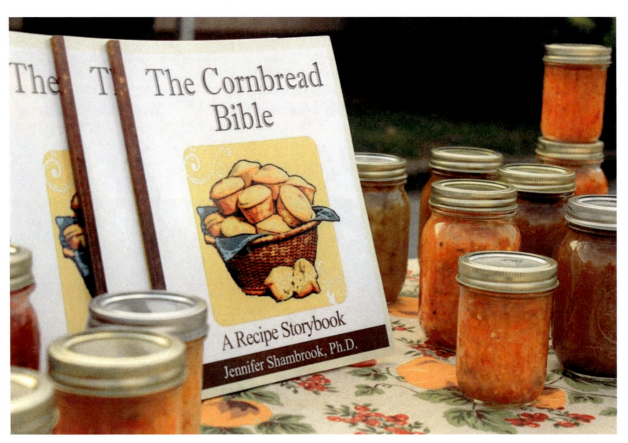

Tracy adopted one of our Maltese puppies for her daughter Michelle to play with. Since she is in Georgia and I am in West Tennessee, my parent's home in north central Alabama seemed like a perfect place to meet and deliver her new little furry bundle of wiggles and puppy kisses. When we met, she brought a little something extra: some of her very fine pear relish. She had some for us to eat there and then, some for my parents' pantry and some for me to take back to Tennessee.

I put the pear relish in my cupboard and my husband, Robert, found it. "What is this?" he asked. I told him it was Tracy McLean's pear relish. He opened the jar and took a taste. "This is mine," he declared and he ate every bit of it himself!

He's not the only one she has turned into a Pear Relish addict. On more than one occasion, while visiting by phone, our conversation has been interrupted by someone pecking on her door to see if she might have just a little more pear relish they could buy. They might have "company coming over" or they wanted to take a jar to someone for a gift.

Tracy's Pear Relish Recipe

This is another recipe where you are going to really appreciate having a food processor handy!

Ingredients

- 12 pounds pears
- 6 large onions (use sweet Vidalias if you can get them)
- 6 red bell peppers
- 6 green bell peppers
- 4 cups granulated sugar
- 1 Tablespoon kosher salt
- 1 Tablespoon allspice
- 5 cups apple cider vinegar

Instructions

1. Peel, core and quarter pears. (You may want to use an apple peeler like the Starfrit Pro Peeler sold on Amazon)
2. Peel and wash onions.
3. Remove stems and seeds from peppers.
4. Measure all other ingredients into a large canning kettle.
5. Finely chop pears, onions, and peppers and adding them to the kettle as you go.
6. After all ingredients are added, heat to a boil, then simmer 40 minutes.
7. Meanwhile, start your boiling water bath and prepare your jars, lids and rings.
8. When relish has finished cooking, fill hot jars with relish, using a canning funnel and canning scoop.
9. Wipe rims of jars with a damp paper towel.
10. Seal with lids and rings.
11. Process in a boiling water bath for 20 minutes.
12. Remove to cooling racks or surface covered with folded towels.

Yield: About 10-12 pints

Jerushy's Tomato Relish

Jerusha Wyatt was born in the Bridgeton Community of Alabama, near what would one day become Birmingham. She married J. H. Lee. He was my grandfather's cousin and also my grandmother's cousin. (Yes, I am from Alabama and my grandparents were 2nd cousins, but back then, in the Bridgeton community, you either married a cousin or you did without.) Jerusha and J.H. were married for 60 years. She died at 82 years old, over a decade before I was born. Despite that, Jerusha Lee was very much a part of my life. As a matter of fact, she was and still is quite well known in and around Leeds, Alabama.

Jerusha Lee did all the things that other country wives did. She kept a kitchen garden, cooked three meals a day on a wood-burning cast iron stove for J.H. and their five children. She would have washed clothes on the back porch or in the yard and hung them on the line. These same clothes she would have mended when they were torn, or sewn new shirts or pants or dresses when they needed to be replaced. She would have carried water from the well for drinking or bathing or cooking or washing dishes.

With all of that work to do, Jerusha Lee distinguished herself by developing a recipe that has been passed down for generations. Jerusha Lee was a neighbor and friend of my great grandmothers Susan Lee DeShazo and Dora Leatherwood Nichols. She taught all of them how to make her relish. They taught their daughters, including my grandmother to make the relish which they called "Jerushy." The recipe passed to my mother's generation, then my generation and now my daughter's generation is all making the tomato relish that goes by her name.

I checked with her great-granddaughter, Linda Lee Waller and her granddaughter, Betty Lee Bailey, to see if anyone had a picture of Jerusha. Betty had the only picture we could find which was taken in the Bold Springs cemetery by J.H.'s grave on Memorial Day. She would have been about 80 at the time, but, as you can see, she still had a head full of long dark hair. So here we are, over a century and a half since she was born and over 70 years since she was laid to rest next to her life's companion, and we are still cooking her recipe and saying her name. I love Jerushy and I love Jerusha Lee, a legendary woman!

Jerushy Recipe

The number and kind of hot peppers you put in this recipe determines the heat. Use your own taste buds to make that decision. Mama made hers a little on the milder side, Cousin Nello made hers with a little more heat. My clever cousin Patricia DeShazo Sydow was the first one I knew to use diced canned tomatoes to make this when she ran out of Jerushy and couldn't get good fresh tomatoes to make a new batch.

Ingredients

- 2 quarts peeled, diced tomatoes (fresh or canned)
- 2 cups onion, chopped or diced
- 2 cups sweet green peppers, chopped (I like to use one green and one yellow)
- 2 stalks celery chopped
- 2 or more chili peppers (optional, to taste)
- 2 cups sugar
- 1/2 cup sorghum molasses
- 3/4 cup apple cider vinegar
- 1 Tablespoon salt

Instructions

1. Peel and dice or chop tomatoes to yield 2 quarts and place in a large stock pot. (If you don't know how to quickly peel tomatoes I've put instructions below.)
2. Dice or chop onions, peppers, and celery then add to tomatoes.
3. Add sugar, molasses, vinegar and salt then stir over medium high heat.
4. Bring to a boil and simmer until thickened, stir occasionally to keep from scorching.
5. When Jerushy begins to thicken, fill boiling water bath canner half full and add clean 6-7 clean pint jars.
6. After the water begins to boil, place jar lids in a small sauce pan and pour boiling water over lids to soften sealing compound.
7. Once the Jerushy Relish has begun to thicken, remove jars from water bath canner using the jar lifter.
8. Fill jars using canning scoop and canning funnel leaving 1/4 inch head space.
9. Wipe jar rim with dampened paper towel.
10. Fit with lids and rings. Adjust rings to finger tight using kitchen towel and oven mit to protect yourself from hot jars.
11. Return to boiling hot water bath.
12. Repeat until all jars are filled.
13. Bring to boil and process 10 minutes.
14. Remove jars from hot water bath and place on cooling racks or several thicknesses of folded towels.

Yield: About 6 or 7 pints.

Pictured below is Jerushy Relish served with field peas, turnip and mustard greens drizzled with Robert's Hot Pepper Sauce, Uncle Terry's Meatloaf made with home-canned Salsa Roja, and cornbread.

How to Easily Peel Tomatoes

Many recipes call for peeled tomatoes. What you don't want to do is peel them with a knife or vegetable peeler. That takes too long and you'll end up throwing away pieces of the tomato along with the peel.

A quick and easy way to peel tomatoes is to plunge them first into boiling water to loosen the skin, then into ice cold water to stop the cooking process. After you do that, the skin will peel right off!

It works best if you core the tomato first. I don't like to see either the stem end or the blossom end of a tomato, so I trim both of those off before I plunge them into the boiling water bath.

I will use a stock pot to create my hot water bath and fill my sink with cold water and ice cubes for the cold water bath. Once the water begins to boil, use a slotted spoon to place the tomato in the boiling water, wait 30 seconds, or until the skin around the core starts to curl, then remove the tomato and plunge it into the cold water bath. After you have finished with the number of tomatoes you need to peel, pick up each tomato and peel the skin off with your fingers. It will slip right off.

Queensland Corn, Tomato & Pineapple Relish

My husband, Robert, is from Queensland, Australia, and grew up in a little outback settlement called Isisford. Isisford today only has a population of about 100 people. When Robert was growing up there, it was more heavily populated as there were about 300 folks back then.

It is a beautiful little town sitting on the Barcoo River. While Isisford may not have many permanent residents, it does have a lot of visitors. The Barcoo is a great place to fish for Yellow Belly. Clancy's Hotel is the ideal location to get a bed, a bath, and an ice cold beverage or two. If you grew up watching Gunsmoke, you'll feel right at home in Clancy's. It looks like the Longbranch Saloon, and the woman that runs it, Kym, is every bit as pretty and kind as Miss Kitty.

We made a trip to Isisford and stayed at Clancy's this summer. We were there in time for the 2013 Isisford Yellow Belly Fishing Competition. There was a fishing contest, of course, but also a whip cracking contest, and tug of war contests, and wool bale rolling contests, and about a thousand people there enjoying the fun, food and festivities. It was so much fun meeting the people that Robert grew up with and hearing stories about him as a boy and stories of his mother and father. We were so thrilled for our two youngest children, Sage and Daisy, to get to see where their Daddy had grown up.

Robert introduced me to a man in the bar at Clancy's one night whose name was Frank Wright. It was one of those wonderful experiences when you meet someone and you immediately connect with heart and mind. Frank is a cut up and a chatter box like me. Once Robert introduced us, he went back to a more serious conversation leaving Frank and I to talk non-stop for about an hour.

Within minutes I learned that he was 88 years old, originally from England, had served in the Royal Navy during World War 2, met and fell in love with a nurse named Nina, and decided to muster out in Australia. He only went back to England once, back in the seventies. He had six children and they had been born boy, girl, boy, girl, boy, girl. He claimed to have orchestrated that all by himself, although I think Miss Nina was probably due some credit. Miss Nina allows him to go to Clancy's for three shots of whisky a day. We talked and joked and had a great time getting to know each other.

After about an hour, there was finally a lull in the conversation. We had run out of steam. I wanted to get him to talk some more so I asked him, "So tell me frankly, Frank, what do you do to entertain yourself when you aren't here at Clancy's drinking whiskey and chatting up women?"

"Well," he said, "you probably won't know anything about this at your age, but I like to bottle the things that grow on my fruit trees or come out of my veggie patch." I knew from my canning friend, Juleen, that "bottling" was what Aussies call canning. Needless to say, the chatter started back up and we had another hour's worth of conversation.

In the end, Robert and I went over to Frank's house to sample some of his canning pantry favorites. He gave us a jar of his Corn, Tomato and Pineapple Relish and a jar of pepper jelly to take with us to snack on during the rest of our trip.

I gave him a signed paperback version of The Cornbread Bible and told him that I was writing a book on relishes. I asked if I could include his recipe. He said he already had a copy of it written down that he had intended to give to his daughter. He said he would make her another copy and that I was very welcome to it.

I asked him who had taught him the recipe and he said it was an old woman from up near Longreach. "You're no spring chicken, Frank. Is she older than you?" I asked.

"Oh yes," he said, "She was REALLY old."

I'm not sure how old she was, considering Frank was 88, and I'm not sure how old this recipe is, but I am sure it's really good after having some with my friend Frank. I thought this recipe was something a little different that you might want to try. I serve it as a condiment for meat or like a sauce for rice. I hope you immediately like it as much as our daughters, Sage and Daisy, immediately liked our dear friend, Frank.

Sage and Daisy giving Frank a cuddle.

Queensland Relish Recipe

Ingredients

- 3 pounds ripe tomatoes
- 2 large onions
- 2 stalks celery
- 1 can (14-15 oz.) whole kernel corn, drained
- 1 can (14-15 oz) crushed pineapple, drained
- 1 1/2 cups sugar
- 2 cups white distilled vinegar
- 1 Tablespoon salt
- 1 1/2 Tablespoon medium curry powder
- 1 Tablespoon mustard powder
- 2 Tablespoons cornstarch.

Instructions

1. Peel and chop tomatoes.
2. Peel and chop onions.
3. Thinly slice celery stalks
4. Place all in stock pot and add drained corn and pineapple. Stir together.
5. Set aside 1/4 cup of the vinegar and the cornstarch.
6. Add remaining 1 3/4 cups vinegar and all other ingredients to the cooking vessel omitting reserved 1/4 cup vinegar and cornstarch.
7. Bring to a boil over high heat, then reduce heat to simmer for one hour.
8. About 20 minutes before the relish has finished cooking, begin to heat your hot water bath canner. Add clean pint jars.
9. When the water begins to boil remove some in a small saucepan. Place lids in the hot water in the small saucepan to soften the sealing compound.
10. After the relish has cooked for an hour, make a paste from the reserved vinegar and cornstarch.
11. Add to simmering relish to thicken, stirring constantly.
12. Using a canning funnel and canning scoop fill hot jars with relish.
13. Wipe rims with a clean, damp paper towel and fit with lids and rings.
14. Place in hot water bath and return to boil.
15. Process in hot water bath for 15 minutes.
16. Using jar lifter, remove processed jars to cooling racks or folded towels to cool.

Yield: about 5 or 6 pints.

Kentucky Ketchup

If you have ever taken a tour of St. Jude Children's Research Hospital, there is a good chance you were guided through those hopeful halls by Lin Ballew. Lin and I became friends soon after I came to St. Jude. She and I worked in the same building, both belonged to the St. Jude Toastmasters Club and share a love for gardening.

Another thing we share is a very deep attachment to our grandmothers. When I told Lin I was putting together a book on relishes, she offered to share recipes from both of her grandmothers. She also shared with me the story of her grandparents and how they all were one family, even before her Mom and Dad were married.

Both her Crawford grandparents and her Russell grandparents were born, raised and died in Graves County, Kentucky. When hard times came, both families migrated north to Detroit to work in the automobile factories. As soon as they had enough money to manage things back home, they would move back to Kentucky. When things got tough again, they would head back up North where there was work. Both families went back and forth separately and together several times.

Both families had boys who were about the same age. They were pals and even joined the Navy together. When they started dating, Jimmy Russell had a girlfriend, but young Mr. Crawford did not. Fortunately, Jimmy also had a younger sister, so they could double date. They had a great time double dating for a while, until Jimmy and his girlfriend broke up. Mr. Crawford proposed and Miss Russell became the young Mrs. Crawford. Lin was the darling granddaughter shared by Pat and Cleo Russell and Rose and Jimmy Crawford, shown below at Lin's parents' wedding. The couples were lifelong friends.

Kentucky Ketchup Recipe

This recipe is actually a letter that was written from Rose Crawford (shown here with husband Pat) to Cleo Russell. It was most likely written when one of the families was in Detroit and the other was back home in Kentucky. I will list the ingredients mentioned in the letter, then give you the letter as the instructions.

Ingredients

- Tomatoes, whatever you have, Lin said Rose used both green and red, depending upon her garden.
- Peppers, both hot and sweet
- Salt
- Vinegar

Instructions

"Well Cleo, I don't have the recipe for the ketchup, for as Jimmy says, 'It takes an old timer to make it!' Ha! I learned how from Laura and then mine don't taste just like hers for, in fact, I don't carry out her way of making it to a T. But here goes the way I do.

"I just take what tomatoes I want or have. Not too large is better, but if I can't do any better I use the big ones. Slice and also slice quite a bit of hot and sweet pepper if you have it, all through it, and salt to taste. Stir salt all through it. Let stand overnight.

"There will be water rise on it after you salt it. Next morning, drain water off real good. Cover with vinegar, heat and seal. Be careful not to get too salty.

"Now I hope these directions don't sound too complicated and you have wonderful luck.

"Bye.

"P.S. It can be made without sweet pepper, but it makes it better."

Take a stab at it and see what you think. I recommend water bath canning 10 minutes for half pints or 15 minutes for pints. Lin serves it with white beans and cornbread as shown on the next page.

Sweet Pepper Relish

Here is a recipe from Lin's other grandmother, Cleo Russell.

Sweet Pepper Relish Recipe

Ingredients

- 12 large green peppers
- 12 large sweet red peppers
- 2 small hot peppers (not more than 1" long)
- 3 Tablespoons salt
- 1 pint boiling water
- 5 small onions chopped fine
- 4 cups vinegar
- 2 cups sugar

Instructions

1. Remove seeds from peppers and chop all peppers together.
2. Pour boiling water over them and let stand 10 minutes.
3. Drain and add chopped onions, vinegar, sugar and salt.
4. Cook for 20 minutes.
5. Seal in clean hot jars while hot.
6. Boiling water bath 10 minutes for half pints, 15 minutes for pints

Yield: 6-8 pints

Caponata – A Mediterranean Eggplant Relish

I love eggplant for a variety of reasons. I love it because it is so versatile. You can dice up eggplant and put it in spaghetti sauce, or casseroles, or vegetable medleys and it will take on the flavors of its neighbors. Eggplant is a very agreeable little vegetable. It is also very resilient in southern gardens. When everything else is pretty much burned out and has run its course, my eggplants are still happy and smiling and offering something for the table in the heat of the summer. It just has a pleasing personality. Can't help but love it.

I love eggplant parmesan and eggplant lasagna and fried eggplant, which reminds me of fried oysters, so I dip it in cocktail sauce. One Thanksgiving, when I was living in Pittsburgh, Mama and Daddy came up from Alabama and we drove across the beautiful rolling hills and pasturelands of Pennsylvania to Philadelphia so we could spend the holiday with my dear cousin Freda Lee Rosenthal. She served an elegant appetizer of caponata eggplant relish on little toasted pieces of Italian bread.

Caponata is flavorful, tasty, and low in calories as well as fat. Caponata and crostini remind me of Freda and that special Thanksgiving we got to spend together. Of course, I guess I have to admit that every thought of Freda fills me with love and makes me smile. I'm so glad God gave us cousins.

This can be served as an appetizer with toasted bread, a snack with crackers, or as a hot or cold side dish with meals. You can add a little interest to your favorite pesto or tomato based pasta sauce by stirring in a couple of heaping spoonfuls of this relish for texture and flavor. You can also use this to top grilled chicken, beef, or fish.

Caponata Recipe

You can chop this by hand, but I prefer to use a food processor for this so that it spreads a little easier.

Ingredients

- 6 cups eggplant, unpeeled, chopped (2 large eggplants will get you there)
- 3 cups onion, chopped
- 2 cups tomatoes, peeled and chopped
- 1 cup sweet peppers, chopped (as usual, I use different colors)
- 1 cup carrots, chopped
- 1 cup celery, chopped
- 1/2 cup calamata olives, chopped
- 1/2 cup green olives, chopped (I use the pimento stuffed ones I usually have on hand)
- 1 small can mushroom stems and pieces, chopped (I use a half pint of home-canned mushrooms)
- 1/2 cup capers
- 2 Tablespoons minced garlic (about 6 large cloves)
- 1/4 cup olive oil
- 1 cup red wine vinegar
- 1 small can tomato paste
- 1/4 cup sugar
- 2 Tablespoons kosher or canning salt
- 1 teaspoon ground black pepper
- 3 Tablespoons dried Italian herb blend
- 3 Tablespoons dried parsley

Instructions

1. Assemble all ingredients. Chop vegetables and set aside.
2. Heat oil in a large dutch oven or stock pot. Saute eggplant, onions, peppers and garlic until the onion becomes transparent and eggplant is lightly browned.
3. Stir in all remaining ingredients and bring to a boil.
4. Lower heat and allow to simmer gently over low heat for one hour, stirring occasionally to keep from sticking. Your house is going to smell like heaven while this is happening.
5. About 20 minutes to a half hour before the caponata has finished simmering, fill your boiling water bath canner to half full and prepare jars, lids and rings. I use pint jars, but you may want to use half pints if you want to give as a hostess gift.
6. Using canning scoop and canning funnel, fill jars leaving 1/2 inch headspace.
7. Wipe rims of jars with a damp paper towel.
8. Seal with lids and rings.
9. Process in a boiling hot water bath canner 10 minutes for half pints and 15 minutes for pints.

Yield: About 8 pints

Branston Pickle

Each of us has something that has to be in our kitchen for our pantry to be complete. Oftentimes, I think we take some of our regional comfort foods for granted until we move somewhere that prohibits having easy access to them. When I moved to Pennsylvania, I sorely missed some of my kitchen staples. I couldn't get Dale's Steak Sauce or Martha White Self-Rising Corn Meal with Hot Rise unless my Mama sent me a care package or I smuggled it back across the Mason-Dixon Line when I went home for a visit.

Of course, there are always trade-offs. While living in Pennsylvania, I learned about those delicious little potato filled pieroghi dumplings, caponata, steak salad, beety eggs, and a whole host of wonderful Amish foods. But I have to say, I still missed some of the comfort food tastes of home.

I know my Australian husband misses his Australian sausage rolls, meat pies, ANZAC biscuits, and Vegemite. My New York friends who have moved South feel absolutely deprived because they can't get a "decent" bagel. My expat German friends feel a sense of loss over the lack of variety in wursts (sausages). Relocated friends from the far western states will practically shed tears while talking about In and Out Burgers.

Branston Pickle is one of the universally "things-held-dear" and missed by my friends from Great Britain. The first time I tried Branston Pickle, I must admit, was only done to be polite. It looked awful and I wasn't exactly sure what I was supposed to do with it. My friend and co-worker, Win Greenshields, invited me to come by her house for a bite to eat before making the costume contest rounds on Halloween somewhere in the late '80s. I was dressed as Miss Yvonne from the Pee Wee Herman Show. I had my hair teased about five inches from my head in every direction and I wore pointy-toed high heels that were also in about the five inch range. My shoes matched the poofy dress I was wearing that someone had either worn to a prom or as a bridesmaid before donating to the Goodwill. It was a deep shade of aqua, as were my eyelids.

When we arrived at Win's house, her husband was going to great extremes to be a proper host. I was Win's "boss," but I really considered myself more as her co-worker than supervisor. We were close, but her Scottish husband wanted to show his respect and hospitality by keeping things a bit formal. This was a visit from the boss. I wanted to do everything I could to put him at ease, but felt a little ridiculous because I was dressed as "the most beautiful woman in Puppetland."

Frank prepared a plate for me that had mostly recognizable things on there. Cheese, pickles, crackers, and slices of fruit, a tiny little sandwich cut like a diamond. With all of that, however was a dollop of something that looked like chopped vegetables soaked in a dark steaksauce. It smelled pretty good, and I asked them what it was. Win cheerfully told me that it was Branston Pickle and that she had been saving the jar to open that night so she could share it with me. It was obviously a thing most precious.

There was no turning back at that point. I would have eaten it if it had been liver… which is saying a LOT in my case. I scooped some of that brown concoction up on a cracker and popped it into my mouth. I followed with a sliver of cheddar cheese to chew with it.

Boy, was I surprised! Not only was it good, it was truly delicious. I understood why she had saved it for a special occasion and I felt very, very honored that she had shared her precious hoarded pickle with me. It was her last jar of Branston pickle. By Thanksgiving, she had lost her struggle with lung cancer and was gone. I loved her so much that her family agreed to allow her ashes to be buried among my family members at Bold Springs Cemetary.

Branston Pickle will forever be linked to my fond memories of my dear friend and co-worker, Win Greenshields.

Fast forward to 2011 and a visit to the home of my new friends Ruth, James and Sophia, who had recently relocated from London to Memphis to join the St. Jude team. Ruth wanted to make some mincemeat pies for her Christmas party. I usually make mincemeat in the fall when apples are plentiful and on sale or free if you know someone with a tree. I told her that I would get some mincemeat to her.

They were very grateful for the mincemeat. Then they mentioned that they wished I could just make Branston Pickle. "I will figure it out," I said with all the determination of someone who fully understood the great importance of such an endeavor. For my old friend Win, and my new friend Ruth, I present to you this reasonable facsimile of the beloved Branston Pickle.

Branston Pickle has been around since 1922. It was named for the little Staffordshire town where it was first manufactured. Although ownership of the pickle manufacturing rights has changed hands over the decades, the name and recipe have remained the same. The only thing that changed is that you can now get the pickle in the original chunk, small chunk, or paste forms. Over 17 million jars is sold every year.

Branston Pickle is often served as a component of pub-grub known as "Ploughman's Lunch." A roll, cheddar or local cheese, Branston Pickle and fruit. It can also be served as an accompaniment for meat, as you would serve chutney.

Of course, the manufacturer, Crosse & Blackwell, hold all of the rights to the "real" Branston Pickle recipe. This is just my attempt to replicate it. So, just to make that clear, we'll call this Sham-Branston Pickle or Shamston Pickle.

Shamston Pickle Recipe

The recipe calls for a rutabaga (a.k.a swede in the U.K.). I grew up eating rutabagas, but they aren't exactly a common root vegetable and you may have trouble finding one. They look like a turnip, only bigger. They are usually covered in wax. I just use a potato peeler to peel them and remove the wax. If you cannot find a rutabaga, substitute about three turnips instead.

Ingredients

- 1 medium rutabaga (swede), peeled and chopped into pieces about 1/2 inch square
- 2 cups carrots, chopped into small pieces (I use skinny or baby carrots)
- 1 small cauliflower, separated into very small flourettes, stems chopped
- 1 large cucumber, seeded, chopped into 1/2 inch pieces
- 2 medium zucchini, with peel, chopped into 1/2 inch pieces
- 3 medium apples, with peel, chopped into 1/2 inch pieces
- 2 onions, peeled, and chopped into 1/2 inch pieces
- 20 sweet pickle midgets, cut into 1/2 inch pieces
- 6 ounces dates, finely chopped
- 6-7 cloves of garlic, peeled and minced
- 1 12-ounce bottle malt vinegar (do NOT substitute any other kind of vinegar)
- 1/2 cup Worcestershire sauce
- 1 cup, very firmly packed, dark brown sugar (about 10 ounces)
- 1 6-ounce can tomato paste
- 1/4 cup lemon juice
- 2 teaspoons kosher or canning salt
- 1 Tablespoon mustard seed (black if you have them)
- 2 teaspoons ground allspice
- 2 teaspoons cayenne pepper
- 1/4 cup cornstarch
- 3/4 cup water
- Kitchen Bouquet (optional) may be added to darken the color

Instructions

1. Chop all of your vegetables and fruit to a roughly uniform size (although the shape will vary)
2. Combine all ingredients except for cornstarch, water, and Kitchen Bouquet in a large stockpot.
3. Stir all ingredients together.
4. Heat to a boil, then reduce heat to a simmer for about 2 hours, stirring occasionally.
5. Mix cornstarch and water to make a paste. Stir into vegetables and continue to stir while sauce thickens.
6. At this point, if you want a darker sauce for the pickle so that it will more closely resemble the original, you may add a caramel coloring agent, like Kitchen Bouquet.
7. Fill prepared half pint jars using canning funnel and canning scoop.

8. Wipe jar rims with damp paper towel. Seal jars with prepared canning lids and rings.
9. Process in boiling water bath for 15 minutes.
10. Remove from boiling water bath using jar lifter to place on cooling racks or surface covered with folded towels.
11. Label and allow to mellow 3 weeks before using.

Yield: 12-16 half pints

Shamston Pickle in shown in the foreground. Cherry tomato and eggplant marinara (from I Can Can Spaghetti Sauce, 2014) in the back.

Salsa Roja – An Easy and Simple Garden Salsa

Everything about salsa is easy. The ingredients are easy to find. Salsa recipes are easy to obtain. There are even salsa canning kits that are sold for folks just starting to can. I have never purchased the kit, but my aim with this recipe was to create something that was as easy as possible without the extra expense of buying a kit.

Salsa is also easy to eat! Just a bag of tortilla chips and a pint on salsa, and you've got a great appetizer or movie night snack. Salsa is wonderful on a cheese omelet. Nachos, tacos, or Fiesta Salad are a quick and tasty and wonderful dinner for your family. If you are fixing food for a crowd, take a pint jar of your canned salsa, and mix it with some fresh chopped tomatoes, onions and cilantro to stretch what you have canned.

The ingredients for salsa are even easy to grow! You could grow a salsa garden along the side of your house or even in containers on an apartment balcony. I do recall my Uncle Rick having trouble growing tomatoes in Arizona because it gets so hot there. Tomatoes can be a little finicky about the temperature. They hate frost and they don't like extreme heat. Peppers are a bit more forgiving about extreme heat as long as you make sure they get plenty to drink. However, the last time I was in Arizona, it was 105 degrees and my cousin Frankie, her husband Doug and Uncle Rick had a beautiful raised bed vegetable garden. I think the trick is to find tomatoes that will best tolerate your climate. When you harvest that big pile of tomatoes and peppers, get some onion, vinegar, cumin and cilantro and make up a batch of this easy, basic salsa to enjoy all year long.

Before I move on to the recipe, let me tell you just a little bit about my Uncle Rick and Aunt Betty. There were six kids in Daddy's family that survived childhood, five boys and a girl. Uncle Rick was the oldest of the six kids. Uncle Rick was the first who left the family nest to join the Navy.

While stationed in California, Uncle Rick met a vivacious, pretty, dark-haired girl named Betty. She was a college student and was like no one he had ever met before. He fell completely head over heels in love with her. She fell for him, too, but she had the presence of mind to know that this cute sailor boy was not living the life she wanted for herself. She let him know what she had in mind for a husband was a man who didn't drink, didn't smoke, loved the Lord, and was active in the church. It was only that man that could give her the life she wanted to live.

Uncle Rick got down on his knees twice. Once to ask the Lord to fill his heart and help him be the devoted Godly man this devoted Godly woman dreamed of as her husband. Then he got on his knees again to ask Betty to marry him. She was always a positive person and truly believed she could see the change in him. She just knew in her heart that their meeting was not a coincidence, but rather divine providence. They were married after knowing each other for only two weeks!

They had two sets of twin girls, Rickie and Ronnie, then Jackie and Frankie. Rickie and Ronnie and I were all born in the same year. Jackie and Frankie were close in age to our cousin Sue Ann. When the six of us got together, we had the best time ever. We played games, laughed, watched movies, and talked for hours. Their door was always open and their happy home was like an ongoing party.

For over fifty years, until the end of their lives, Uncle Rick and Aunt Betty were an example to others of how a loving married couple could be supportive friends in times of trouble and playful lovers with a deep love and fascination for one another that continued to grow. Of course they had the sad moments life can bring, but they faced those moments together as partners and helped one another through it. They trusted God and loved each other and are a living example that love at first sight is real and can last a lifetime!

Salsa Roja Recipe

The great thing about making your own salsa is that you can adjust the heat of the peppers in your salsa to your own taste. You can make multiple batches at different levels of heat, or you can make it all mild and serve it with hot sauce or chopped hot peppers on the side. You can even make it atomic hot and watch your friends break out in beads of sweat as they demonstrate their courageous heat tolerance. It's your choice. This recipe is what I consider to be medium, but you can up the pepper ante to your own ideal level of heat. I use whatever peppers I happen to have growing in my garden at the time my tomatoes are ripe.

When handling hot peppers, it's a good idea to wear disposable food service gloves.

Ingredients
- 4 lbs tomatoes, peeled and chopped (about 6 cups)
- 3 chopped onions (about 3-4 cups)
- 1 chopped sweet bell pepper (about 1 cup)
- 6 cloves of garlic, minced (about 6 teaspoons)
- half a cup of chopped fresh cilantro or 3 tablespoons dried cilantro
- Hot peppers, chopped, to taste (in my last batch I used 2 jalapeno, 2 mild Anaheim, and two chili peppers, including seeds.)
- 1 heaping teaspoon powdered cumin
- 2 teaspoons canning salt or kosher salt
- 1 cup vinegar (white distilled or apple cider)

Instructions
1. This recipe goes together quickly, so go ahead and start your hot water bath and prepare your jars. This will make about 5 pints with a little left over to eat right away. Have some chips handy.
2. Wash and assemble your ingredients. As you chop each ingredient, add it to the pot that you are going to cook it in.
3. After adding all chopped fresh ingredients, sprinkle with the remaining ingredients and then pour the vinegar over all.
4. Stir together. (I warn you, this is going to smell so good that you are going to need a good bit of will power here to keep from eating the entire pot at this point. Be strong.)
5. Heat to boiling, then lower heat and simmer 10 minutes, stirring occasionally.
6. Remove some water from the boiling water bath canner to pour over canning lids in order to soften sealing compound.
7. Remove jars from water bath canner using jar lifter.
8. Using canning funnel and canning scoop, fill jars leaving 1/4 inch head space.
9. Place jars in boiling water bath and return to boil.
10. Process jars in boiling water bath for 15 minutes.
11. Use jar lifter to remove from canner and place on cooling racks or folded towels to cool.

Yield: About 5 pints.

Uncle Terry's Mexican Meatloaf Recipe

I recently had the honor of being asked to be the keynote speaker at the Alabama Farmer's Federation Heritage Cooking Contest in Montgomery, Alabama. Their theme for 2013 was cornbread, so they asked me to come talk about some of the stories in The Cornbread Bible: A Recipe Storybook.

My Uncle Terry and Aunt Glenda live down in that part of the Great State of Alabama, so they blessed my heart by coming to hear my talk. After the talk was over, Uncle Terry came over and handed me this recipe. He said that at his house, he always had to make the meatloaf because his was the family favorite. Since it is made with salsa, I wanted to include it here so you can try it with your canned salsa.

Ingredients:
- 1 pound extra lean ground beef
- 1 egg
- 1 slice of bread soaked in milk
- 2/3 to 3/4 cup salsa, more or less
- Season with salt, pepper and garlic powder to taste
- Cooking spray or a little olive oil on a paper towel
- Ketchup to go on top as it bakes

Instructions:
1. Preheat oven to 400*F
2. Rub your loaf pan with olive oil or spray with cooking spray
3. Put your bread in a bowl big enough to mix your meatloaf.
4. Pour in enough milk to soak the bread (1/4-1/3 cup)
5. Add remaining ingredients.
6. Mix together well (I wear food handler gloves and use my fingers)
7. Pat into a loaf pan that has been treated with cooking spray or rubbed with a little oil.
8. Top with ketchup.
9. Bake one hour at 400*F
10. Let rest 10 minutes before slicing to serve.

Uncle Terry and Aunt Glenda caught smooching right in front of the grandkids! Still sweethearts!

Salsa Verde Southern Style – Made with green tomatoes

When you can from your garden, it's really nice when the tomatoes are ripe at the same time the peppers are ready. Sometimes it turns out that way and sometimes it doesn't. When I had an abundance of peppers, but only green tomatoes, it occurred to me to make Salsa Verde with green tomatoes. I love green tomatoes and I love salsa… there had to be a way to make this work.

Salsa Verde is Spanish for green salsa. It is traditionally made with tomatillos rather than tomatoes. Tomatillos have always been a little suspect to me. They look a little peculiar because they have that little papery cover over their "real" skin. They also cost a small fortune, if you can even find them in the produce section of your market. If you do find them, pay the small fortune, peel away the papery little baby blanket and cut into it you will discover the same thing I did: Tomatillos are just some kind of fancy little dressed-up green tomatoes with a Hispanic accent.

It was with those thoughts swirling around in my brain that I came up with this recipe and started swirling around in my kitchen to get some of this in my pantry. You can make your green salsa hot and your red salsa mild as a way to color code for heat levels. When you want a little green salsa to go with the red for a mouth-watering Mexican dish, pull a jar of this out of your cabinet.

Salsa Verde Southern Style Recipe

Ingredients

- 2 lbs green tomatoes, chopped (you can leave the skin on these)
- 2 onions, chopped
- 1 sweet bell pepper, chopped (pick a pretty color)
- Hot peppers to taste, sliced thin (I used 6 chilies, red and green)
- 4 cloves garlic, minced (about 4 teaspoons)
- 1/3 cup fresh cilantro, chopped fine, or 2 Tablespoons dried
- 1 teaspoon cumin
- 1/2 teaspoon kosher or pickling salt
- 1/2 cup fresh squeezed lime juice (2-3 limes, watch to remove seeds)
- 1 cup white distilled vinegar
- 1/2 cup water

Instructions

1. Start your hot water bath and prepare your jars. This will make about 3 pints or 6 half pints. Think about how much you are likely to eat on one occasion to decide which jars you will use.
2. Wash and assemble your ingredients. As you chop each ingredient, add it to the pot that you are going to cook it in.
3. Sprinkle cilantro, cumin and salt over chopped vegetables.
4. Squeeze enough juice from limes to make 1/2 cup. Add to seasoned vegetables.
5. Pour vinegar and water over all and stir together well.
6. Heat to boiling, then lower heat and simmer 15 minutes, stirring occasionally.
7. Remove some water from the boiling water bath canner to pour over canning lids in order to soften sealing compound.
8. Remove jars from water bath canner using jar lifter.
9. Using canning funnel and canning scoop, fill jars leaving 1/4 inch head space.
10. Place jars in boiling water bath and return to boil.
11. Process jars in boiling water bath for 15 minutes.
12. Use jar lifter to remove from canner and place on cooling racks or folded towels to cool.

Yield: About 3 pints or 6 half pints

Hungarian Pepper Mustard Sauce

I belong to an online canning forum on Spark People. We help each other maintain a healthy lifestyle and swap stories and recipes and gardening tips. The leader of the group is Patti Habbyshaw. She is a great leader and keeps us all motivated with her adventures on her 17 acre homestead in the Midwest.

When I told her I was doing this book, she said I should try out her Hungarian Pepper Mustard Sauce to see if it would be a good fit for the book. She makes this sauce and barters with it at the Farmer's Market. I love a recipe that is easy to make. I love a recipe that has inexpensive ingredients, I love a recipe that has bold flavor. I love a recipe that helps me get dinner on the table with ease. Any one of those criteria will have me in the kitchen chopping and peeling and boiling water and washing jars. This recipe has ALL of those criteria met! On top of all of that, it is absolutely beautiful in the jars. It looks like confetti in sunshine.

When I read the recipe, I thought, this would make a great sauce for baking chicken breasts. When I asked Patti what she did with it, this is what she said: "A ton!!! Not only is it great on hamburgers and hot dogs, but great as a basting sauce for grilled chicken or pork tenderloin. Baste the last few minutes of grilling, just enough time to let it char and caramelize a bit. Also, when doing breaded oven baked anything, use the mustard instead of the egg and flour. It will hold the breading to the meat and flavor the meat with the mustard and pepper flavor. You can also mix it with sour cream or yogurt to use as a pretzel or veggie dip. Add it to any casserole for a boost of flavor. I also add it to my homemade gravy, pot roast, or when making a Chinese recipe. Go ahead and be creative!"

Does that not make you want to just put this book down and head out to the kitchen to start canning right now?!? I had the recipe less than 24 hours before I had made a batch! This is definitely going to be one of my annual pantry staples. From now on, when the banana peppers start coming in, you'll find me somewhere buying a quart of mustard!

Hungarian Pepper Mustard Sauce Recipe

Hungarian wax peppers are what we call banana peppers in the South. The proper Hungarian Wax Peppers come in varying levels of heat. You can add some hot peppers to sweet peppers if you want to add a little heat to your sauce. Adjust it for how you plan to use the sauce and for whom you are going to be cooking.

Ingredients

- 8 cups finely chopped banana peppers in various colors (about 50 peppers)
- 1 quart yellow prepared mustard
- 1 quart distilled white vinegar
- 5 cups granulated sugar
- 1 cup flour
- 3/4 cup water

Instructions

1. Start your boiling water bath and prepare your jars and lids. This cooks up pretty fast.
2. Trim stems from peppers and finely chop with food processor, including seeds.
3. Mix first four ingredients in a large stock pot. Bring to a boil, then lower heat and simmer for 20 minutes, stirring occasionally.
4. Mix flour and water into a smooth paste. Stir into mustard and pepper mixture.
5. Stir and allow to cook until thickened.
6. Using a canning funnel and scoop, fill jars, wipe rims, and seal with lids and rings.
7. Process in a boiling water bath for 20 minutes.

Yield: Makes 9 pints

Australian Red Onion Relish

Another member of my online canning group is Juleen Dickins. Juleen lives in Australia, down south in the cooler regions of Victoria. Juleen shared this recipe with me and I knew before I ever made it that I was going to love it. Juleen's seasons are just the opposite of mine so she is working on her winter garden while I am trying to keep my plants well watered to prevent the heat of the summer from drying my garden out. But despite being on opposite sides of the world and in different hemispheres, we share a lot in common. We both love canning, sauces, mushrooms and red onions.

There is just something about red onions. Intellectually, I know that if I closed my eyes and you put some red onion and some yellow onion and some white onion on a dish, I probably would not be able to distinguish between them. But in my internal onion hierarchy, white trumps yellow, and red trumps white. I don't know what it is, but red onions just seem a bit more festive.

This relish is wonderful on any kind of meat, but I save it especially to have with canned Amish meatloaf (the recipe is in I Can Can Ground Meats, which is due to be published just a few weeks after this book.) One of my favorite quick meals is canned Amish Meatloaf smothered in Juleen's Red Onion Relish, home-canned white beans or home-canned carrots. I can go from the pantry to sitting at the table in about fifteen minutes with a delicious meal. I wish you could just smell this…. it is soooo good!

Red Onion Relish Recipe

You could make this with white or yellow onions if you prefer. I won't tell a soul!

Ingredients

- 1 Tablespoon olive oil
- 2 cloves garlic, crushed (more if you like a stronger flavor)
- 1 bay leaf
- 4 large red onions sliced and separated into rings or chopped finely
- 1 cup brown sugar
- 1/2 cup red wine vinegar
- 1 teaspoon salt (or to taste)
- 1/2 teaspoon black pepper (or to taste)

Instructions

1. Start boiling water bath canner and prepare half pint jars and lids.
2. Heat oil in dutch oven and cook onion slowly until soft. It should not brown.
3. Add all remaining ingredients and bring to a fast simmer.
4. Stir and reduce heat to gently cook uncovered for about 20 minutes or until liquid has reduced to your liking.
5. Taste and adjust seasonings and perhaps sugar if it is too vinegary.
6. Spoon into prepared jars and seal with lids and rings.
7. Process in a boiling water bath for 10 minutes for half pints, 15 minutes for pints.
8. Remove to cooling racks or towel-covered surface to cool.

Yield: 4-5 half pints

Home Canned Barbecue Sauce

Honestly, I debated whether or not to even add a recipe for barbecue sauce. You can buy so many good barbecue sauces at the store AND there are so many regional barbecue sauce variations. Mine is tomato based, thick, sweet and vinegary with a little heat. In the Carolinas, they would demand more mustard. Elsewhere there would be a preference for less heat or sweetness. This sauce will please some and down-right offend others. But this is what we like in our neck of the woods.

Besides, I was afraid I might actually be violating some sort of sacred Southern code if I, as a Southern gal, were to publish a book on sauces and NOT include at least one recipe for barbecue sauce. For decades, my family has had a big family reunion down by the Coosa River at my Daddy's lake lot. There would be, literally, over a hundred family

members in attendance. Uncle Lee would sit up all night roasting a whole pig on a spit over an open hickory fire. That stopped over a decade ago when Uncle Lee was no longer able to do it.

My cousin, Maurice, decided to revive the practice a couple of years ago. I warned him that it was a HUGE amount of work and took a really long time. He was adventurous, though, and determined to have a roast pig for the family pow-wow. Aunt Mary Ellen has a homestead and she supplied the pig. It was quite a learning experience. Maurice DID successfully roast the pig, and it was delicious, but it was also not done until about four o'clock, rather than time for the meal at noon. It made us all just that much more appreciative of how hard Uncle Lee had worked to have that pig ready on time for all those years. And, Maurice got to check roasting a whole pig over an open fire off his bucket list. In the picture below, two pigs are being prepared for roasting over a hickory fire. Norma Jean, in the blue shirt chopped all of the hickory from trees that had fallen during a tornado.

Barbecue Sauce Recipe

I have adapted this old recipe for use with convenient modern kitchen appliances

Ingredients
- 2 dozen red tomatoes (enough to make about a gallon when chopped)
- 2 large onions
- 3-4 stalks celery
- 2 large red sweet bell peppers
- 4 or 5 hot peppers (adjust to taste)
- 4-5 cloves garlic, finely minced
- 1 cup firmly packed dark brown sugar
- 1/4 cup sorghum molasses
- 2 teaspoons ground peppercorns (I like to use multi-color)
- 1 Tablespoon Paprika (I like smoky Hungarian)
- 1 Tablespoon Kosher or Canning Salt
- 1/2 teaspoon cayenne pepper
- 1/3 cup prepared mustard
- A few dashes of Liquid Smoke (optional) if you would like a hickory flavor
- 1 cup apple cider vinegar (you can also use a fruit or herb flavored vinegar for a different taste)

Instructions
1. Core, peel, and quarter tomatoes.
2. Trim and discard leaves from celery and rough chop for food processor.
3. Peel, wash, and cut onions into quarters, then cut quarters in half.
4. Cut sweet peppers in half, remove seeds and stems then cut each half into quarters.
5. Rough chop hot peppers, discard stems. (Remove seeds if you want to lower heat.)
6. With all vegetables prepared for food processor. Chop in batches to a very fine chop. You want to end up with a puree.
7. Place the vegetable mixture in a large pot and bring to a boil.
8. Reduce heat to medium and simmer for about an hour, or until the mixture has cooked down until is about half of what you had to start with.
9. You can put your sauce through a sieve at this point, if you want to remove the seeds, or just keep on going if you don't mind the seeds.
10. Pour sauce into a slow-cooker and add all of the remaining ingredients
11. Cook on high for 4 hours or on low for 8-10 hours.
12. Prepare hot water bath, canning jars, lids and rings.
13. Using a canning scoop or ladle into prepared jars and seal with lids and rings.
14. Process in a boiling water bath for 20 minutes for both half pints or pints.
15. Remove to cooling racks or towel-covered surface to cool.

Yield: 4-5 pints

Chutney: A Shambrook Family Fave

Lamb roast is one of my husband's all time favorite meals. He also loves roast beef or roast venison. We cook our roasts with potatoes, carrots, onions, celery, summer or winter squash, sweet peppers, and eggplant. Not only does he love to eat them, he loves to cook them, so about once a month I will be surprised with the delicious smell of roast and vegetables when I arrive home from work. Our ever helpful little girls set the table. My only chore on those nights is to open a jar of chutney.

The whole family loves to eat our roasts with home-canned chutney. We can easily go through a half pint jar in one meal. We put it on top of the sliced roast rather than gravy.

I use apples and dried fruits for my chutney, but you can use pears if that is what you have on hand, or a mixture of the two.

Chutney Recipe

I've also included a recipe after this one that I use for making Cran-Apple Jelly from the peels and cores from the chutney. I make the juice while I'm chopping the apples and getting the chutney together, then make the jelly while the chutney is simmering.

To peel your apples, I recommend the Starfrit Apple Pro Peeler. I ordered one from Amazon and I absolutely love it. It can peel five apples faster than I could peel one by hand. It is less than $20 and looks like a toy, but that thing is better than one of the shoemaker's elves for getting work done for you!

Ingredients
- 15-20 tart apples
- 1 pound of golden raisins
- 1 pound dark raisins
- 1 cup dried cranberries (like Craisins)
- 1 cup dried chopped dates
- 2 cups chopped onion
- 1 chopped sweet red pepper
- 1 chopped green bell pepper
- 2 cloves garlic, minced
- 1 Tablespoon red pepper flakes (or chopped hot pepper, to taste)
- 4 cups brown sugar
- 3 Tablespoons mustard seed
- 2 Tablespoons ground ginger
- 2 teaspoons curry powder
- 2 teaspoons salt

Instructions
1. Peel and core apples (Note: If you are going to make apple peel and core jelly, go ahead and throw the peels in the pot with water to start making your juice. You can have a batch of jelly done before the chutney finishes cooking!)
2. Chop apples into chunks that are roughly a half inch or less
3. Place all ingredients into a stock pot and mix together well.
4. Bring to a boil, then reduce heat to simmer on a low heat for 90 minutes, stirring occasionally to keep the chutney from sticking to the bottom of the pot. The chutney will thicken as it cooks.
5. Start your boiling water bath and prepare jars and lids about a half hour before the chutney has finished simmering.
6. Fill hot jars leaving 1/4 inch head space. Seal with canning jar lids and rings.
7. Process in a hot water bath for 10 minutes.
8. Using jar lifter, remove to cooling racks or surface covered with folded towels.

Yield: About 10 - 12 pints

Cran-Apple Jelly from peelings and cores

Making jelly from cores and peels makes me feel like I'm getting away with something. I hope you find it just as satisfying!

I was raised to always be a good steward of whatever I had. I save empty plastic food containers. I was recycling when it was considered "tacky" rather than "cool." If there is a leftover bit of something, it goes in the freezer to wait until time to make soup. If I get a good deal on something, I drag out my canning jars… you already know that. So you won't be surprised that I don't like throwing away apple cores and peels.

For those of you who have chickens, don't feel obligated to deprive your little feathered friends of a delicious apple core and peel feast on chutney making day. For those that don't have feathered friends, here is a great recipe to make the best use of those cores and skins. And, for those who have feathered friends and like apple jelly well enough to tell the hens to go back to pecking bugs in the yard, this is for you, too!

Ingredients

- Peels and cores from 15-20 tart apples
- 6 cups water
- 1 box powdered pectin
- 9 cups sugar
- 1-2 cups Cranberry juice (I like to use Cranberry-Pomegranate)

Instructions

1. Place peels, cores and water in a large pot. Bring to a boil, then lower heat. Simmer, covered, for one half hour.
2. Strain juice through a strainer lined with coffee filters or cheesecloth, or use a jelly bag.
3. Start boiling water bath canner and prepare jars while juice is straining.
4. Measure apple juice and add enough cranberry juice to make 7 cups.
5. Return to pot, add pectin, stir in well and bring to a rapid boil.
6. Add sugar. Return to a rapid boil. Boil, stirring constantly for 1-2 minutes.
7. Skim foam if necessary.
8. Using canning funnel and canning scoop, pour into prepared jars, leaving 1/8 inch headspace.
9. Wipe rims and seal with prepared canning jar lids and rings.
10. Process in a boiling water bath 5 minutes.
11. Using jar lifter, remove jars to cooling racks or towel covered surface to cool.

Yield: 10-12 half pints.

Cranberry-Orange Relish with Triple Sec – An everyday holiday

Let me go ahead and say up front that I think store-bought jellied cranberry sauce is, in my opinion, is a nasty looking, artificial tasting, liver-colored, embarrassment on a holiday table. Let me be even more opinionated and say that you should either make your own cranberry sauce (which is probably the easiest recipe in this book) or just leave it off the menu altogether.

Now that I have that bit of tactless rudeness off my chest, let me ask for your forgiveness, if I have offended you. Please know I said it out of love for you and your Thanksgiving guests. It was for your own good. Once you make this recipe, you will be a convert and preach the home-made cranberry relish gospel right alongside me, I am sure!

There are a lot of wonderful things about this recipe. First of all, if you get your cranberries when they go on sale, you can make up a big batch for next to nothing! This makes a great gift and it is also a great farmer's market choice if you are canning relish to take to market. Best of all, you can have this festive relish all year long! You don't have to wait for a holiday.

You can grab a rotisserie chicken, a box of stuffing mix and a can of green beans at the store then add this beautiful relish and you have an everyday holiday meal. Even better yet, if you have a well stocked pantry and freezer, you can pull a pint of home canned chicken (a la I Can Can Chicken) and a frozen pan of dressing (a la The Cornbread Bible) with a jar of home canned carrots, or field peas, or green beans, and you've got dinner from your own stores of home-prepared food in minutes. Add the home-canned cranberry sauce, and you will have a meal that will have your family grinning at their plates as they sincerely thank the Lord while they say the blessing.

Cranberry-Orange Relish with Triple Sec Recipe

I like the little zip the Triple Sec adds to this. It is like an extract. Yes, it has some alcohol in it, just like vanilla extract, but the alcohol burns off as it cooks, so don't worry about the alcohol content if that is a concern for you or someone that eats at your table. It is just in there for the delicious orangey flavor of the Triple Sec. If you want to omit the Triple Sec or just have a batch with a bit of a different flavor, just substitute orange juice and a teaspoon of almond extract.

For those of you that aren't practicing alcohol abstinence, if you have Triple Sec left over, this is one of the ingredients for "real" margaritas. You might just want to keep that in mind if you make one of the salsa recipes. Waste not, want not.

This recipe can be easily doubled or tripled if you want to make a larger batch. I make this in both half pints for family dinners and gifts and pints for larger gatherings.

Ingredients

- 12 cups cranberries, washed (3 pounds)
- 6 cups sugar
- 2 oranges
- 3 cups water
- 2 cups orange juice
- 1 cup Triple Sec

Instructions

1. Fill your water bath canner half full, add jars and prepare lids with hot water to soften sealing compound.
2. Rinse berries and pick through to be sure you've removed any of the little stems that might have found their way into the bag.
3. Place washed berries in a stock pot.
4. Measure and pour in sugar.
5. Grate the zest from the oranges into the berries and sugar.
6. Remove the white pith from the orange and section the oranges.
7. Chop oranges and add to berries.
8. Add water and orange juice.
9. Heat to boiling, stirring constantly.
10. Add Triple Sec. Return to boil, then reduce heat to simmer.
11. Simmer, stirring frequently to keep from boiling over, for 10 minutes.
12. Turn off heat. Remove jars from boiling water bath and fill jars leaving 1/4 inch headspace using canning scoop and funnel.
13. Wipe rims and add lids and rings.
14. Process in boiling water bath for 10 minutes

Yield: About 6 pints, or 12 half pints, or 3 pints and 6 half pints… you get the idea…

German Red Cabbage – It was Fascination

From a very early age, I have had a fascination with Germany. My family has had many strong ties with der Fatherland. My earliest recollections would be with visits to my Uncle George and Aunt Margot's apartment in the Southside of Birmingham. Uncle George brought Aunt Margot home from Germany after he had served there in the military. When I saw *Breakfast at Tiffany's,* I thought Audrey Hepburn was wonderful because she looked like my Aunt Margot. They had a son, Maurice, whose age was sandwiched between me (1955) and my brother (1958). They also had a cute little baby named Sonja. They moved to Colorado when we were all still little kids, but visited Alabama occasionally, and I visited them in Colorado when my husband was stationed there in the Air Force. (Hugging Maurice below.)

The flame of fascination was fanned a bit more by watching Shirley Temple play Heidi, then reading the book. Then my cousin Jeannie Brooks, Aunt Lorraine's daughter, moved back to Leeds after living in Germany when we were in the middle school years. My cousin, Holly, went to Germany to live and sent a beautiful carved Cuckoo Clock to Granny Tom and Papa Jack to remind us of her living in Germany every hour on the hour and half-hour. My cousin, Cindy, married a young man who was a first generation American of German imigrants. Cindy learned from her mother-in-law to make the best German Potato Salad I have ever eaten!

I acted on that fascination by joining the Army and volunteering to go to Germany, where I served for 14 months. I loved the food and wine and beer and culture. I went back again a few years later as an Air Force wife and lived there for another two years. I even learned to speak the language well enough that I was able to go right into German 104 when I was using my G.I. Bill to get my Bachelor of Arts degree.

Some of the foods I really loved were Sauerbraten, Jagerschnitzel, Chateau Briand (which is a French dish that was very common in the Kaiserslautern region), many kinds of wursts (sausages), several potato dishes, and especially their red cabbage. You should see the size of the cabbages they grow over there! It was nothing to see a wagon being pulled behind a tractor on a country road that was loaded down with cabbages the size of a basketballs!

That is also where I learned about intensive gardening and community gardens. Germany is a beautiful country. If it is not on your bucket list, you might want to revise your list to include Germany. If you go, don't just spend time in the cities, head out to the countryside, that's where the true beauty of the country can be found. Stop in a little village Gasthaus for lunch or dinner and try something that is served with red cabbage (rot kohl). You will love it, if you do!

You can find pickled red cabbage in the grocery store, but it usually has a pretty dear price attached to it. A one-and-a-half pint jar is about five dollars. For about the same amount of money, you can make around five quarts. I will open a quart and keep it in the refrigerator and use it either cold, like a salad, or heat it for a side dish. When serving for a side dish, mix about a cup and a half to two cups it with about a tablespoon of flour mixed into a half cup of water and added to the cabbage as you heat it on top of your stove. This makes the sauce a bit thicker and gives it a bit of a different texture.

Warm red cabbage, bratwurst, and German potato salad with some Hungarian Pepper Mustard and a firm textured roll is an easy and delicious German meal for your family or guests. If you want to make German Potato Salad, or any other kind of potato salad, in a flash, having canned potatoes on hand will help. I recommend taking a look at *Canned Potatoes and Recipes* by Pamela Ritter, if you're interested in canning potatoes. You can often get potatoes at a huge discount when you buy in bulk and they are very handy for having on hand for your starch when you want to put together a healthy family meal in minutes.

German Red Cabbage Recipe

I use a food processor to shred the cabbage which works like a dream. You can also use a mandolin (be careful!!) or even shred with a sharp knife, but it will take a while. I especially love to use the food processor for red cabbage because it cuts uniform shreds and makes the work go quickly.

I use shredded cabbage, but you could also chop the cabbage, if that is what you prefer. Just pick the one you think is the prettiest or easiest to you.

Ingredients
- 8 lbs red cabbage, shredded (or chopped very finely)
- 1/2 cup salt (about 1 Tablespoon per pound of cabbage)
- 2 quarts red wine vinegar
- 1 pound brown sugar
- 1/3 cup mustard seed (yellow or black)
- 1/4 cup celery seed
- 1 teaspoon ground cinnamon
- 1 teaspoon ground cloves
- 1 teaspoon ground allspice
- 1/4 teaspoon nutmeg
- 1 teaspoon freshly ground black peppercorns

Instructions
1. Remove any dry or damaged outer leaves, rinse and shred (or chop) cabbage
2. Place cabbage in a large container and salt in layers as you are shredding and adding to the large container. Cabbage will begin to wilt from the salt.
3. Mix all cabbage and salt together very well.
4. Cover and let stand in a cool, dry place overnight up to 24 hours
5. Pour cabbage into a large colander and rinse lightly to remove some of the salt, allow to drain
6. Start boiling water bath full enough to cover the size jars you are using
7. Prepare jars and heat lids in order to soften sealing compound
8. In a large stockpot, heat vinegar, sugar and spices
9. Heat to boiling and boil, stirring to dissolve sugar, reduce heat and simmer 5 minutes
10. Place well drained cabbage in stockpot and stir well to thoroughly mix spiced vinegar with cabbage.
11. Bring to a boil, stirring, and simmer 5 minutes.
12. Turn off heat and pack into pint or quart jars using canning funnel and canning scoop leaving 1/4 inch head space.
13. Wipe rims and add prepared lids and rings.
14. Process in a boiling water bath for 20 minutes.
15. Remove from bath using a jar lifter and place on cooling racks or surface covered with folded towels.

Yield: 5 quarts

Asian Plum Sauce for Zhang Xiao Yun Johnson

My cousin, Christopher Johnson, made an interesting and adventurous choice when he graduated from Auburn University. He wanted see a little bit of the world, so he went to China to work for a while before settling down with a job close to home. Little did he know that he had taken the first step to the most wonderful adventure of his life. While he was in China, he met a stunningly beautiful young woman named Zhang Xiao Yun. They fell so in love that Yun agreed to follow Chris back to America to become his wife. At the time I am writing this, they are on their honeymoon. She is my newest cousin, so I wanted to put something in this book to welcome her to the family.

Just like my new cousin, Yun, this sauce is sweet and a little spicy. It makes a great dipping sauce for egg rolls or spring rolls. You can also serve it with chicken or duck. It also makes a delicious glaze for clove studded ham. Unless you think you will use a pint at a time, you may want to can this in half-pint jars.

Asian Plum Sauce Recipe

This is a delicious all natural alternative to the dye-filled sauces offered at the grocery store.

I use the food processor for this, however you can hand chop if you prefer.

Ingredients

- 3 pounds plums, washed and pits removed
- 3/4 cup chopped onion
- 1 clove garlic, finely chopped
- 2 cups brown sugar, firmly packed
- 1 cup granulated sugar
- 2 teaspoons ground ginger
- 1/2 teaspoon ground mustard
- 2 teaspoons salt
- 2 cups apple cider vinegar

Instructions

1. Wash plums, cut in half and remove pit. Cut into quarters.
2. Roughly chop a peeled, washed onion that will yield approximately 3/4 cup of finely chopped onion.
3. Peel and roughly chop garlic.
4. Add about a fourth of the plums, onions, and garlic to the food processor bowl with the chopping blade fitted.
5. Chop the ingredients together and empty into a cooking vessel.
6. Continue combining and chopping onion, garlic and plums until all have been chopped and added to the cooking vessel.
7. Add all remaining ingredients and stir together over medium high heat until sugar dissolves. Bring to a boil, then lower heat and simmer for 30 minutes, stirring occasionally.
8. Fill hot water bath canner half full of water and place on heating element.
9. Place 8 clean half-pint jars in the hot water bath canner as it is heating.
10. When the water begins to boil, remove some of the water with a small saucepan. Place the jar lids in the saucepan to soften the sealing compound.
11. When the Asian Plum Sauce is ready, remove jars with a jar lifter.
12. Fill each jar leaving 1/4 inch head space.
13. Wipe jar rims and seal with lid and ring.
14. Repeat until all jars are filled.
15. Place jars in boiling hot water bath and process for 20 minutes.

Yield: 10 half pints

Robert's Hot Pepper Sauce *(from The Cornbread Bible: A Recipe Storybook)*

Below is the method we use at the Shambrook house. I taught my Australian husband, Robert, to make pepper sauce and he makes it for the family now. He has entered it into competition in both South Carolina and Tennessee and has won Blue Ribbons and Best of Show for his pepper sauce.

I like the pepper-infused vinegar for my greens. Robert likes to eat the peppers. We are just like Jack Spratt who could eat no fat and his wife who could eat no lean. So between the two of us, we lick the jars quite clean!

NOTE: When working with hot peppers, use gloves if you have them, or wash your hands thoroughly after handling the peppers. Don't touch any part of your body that might be delicate enough to be burned by the pepper juice (e.g., mouth, eyes, nose, open cuts, etc…. especially your etc.)

Robert's Hot Pepper Sauce Recipe

Ingredients
- Enough hot peppers to fill whatever cute little bottle or jar you want to use.
- White distilled or apple cider vinegar – also enough to fill the jar.

Instructions
1. Stab each of the peppers with a sharp knife. This will allow the vinegar to fill the cavity of the pepper and absorb the heat from the seeds.
2. Fill a pretty little container with the hot peppers.
3. Put enough apple cider or white distilled vinegar into a glass mixing cup to fill the container of peppers (remember we are going to be filling the cavities, too.)
4. Heat to a vicious rolling boil in the microwave.
5. Using a funnel, pour the hot vinegar over the peppers. Let settle, shake, to encourage air pockets to rise.
6. Heat more vinegar and fill again.
7. Repeat filling, settling, shaking and refilling until the vinegar level stops dropping (usually about 3 or 4 times, in my experience.)
8. Allow the pepper sauce to ferment, unrefrigerated, for 2-3 days.

Fiesta Salad from I Can Can Beef

Ingredients

- 1 pint home canned beef cubes
- 1 teaspoon cumin
- 1 Tablespoon chili powder (like Mexene)
- 1 teaspoon garlic powder
- 1 bag restaurant style tortilla chips
- Chopped iceberg lettuce (or a small bag of salad mix)
- 4 oz. shredded cheese
- 1 jar salsa *(you can use your Salsa Roja or Salsa Verde Southern Style here!)*
- 1 small container either guacamole or sour cream
- 1 small onion diced
- 1 small tomato diced
- Chopped olives (optional)

Instructions

1. Pour the meat with juices into a small saucepan, sprinkle with spices, and heat to a boil. Turn down to low after the meat and juices reaches boiling and allow to simmer to blend flavors while you create your salad assembly line.
2. Line up your plates so you can easily assemble each plate.
3. Start with the tortilla chips. I try to arrange them so that there are points pointing out around the edges. It makes the chips easy to grab. Over the chips, create a bed of lettuce on each plate.
4. Divide the meat and juice over each bed of lettuce. Don't forget the juice, it really makes the salad taste great!
5. Sprinkle the cheese over the hot meat, then top with a salsa (I use 2 or 3 spoonfuls).
6. In the middle of the salsa, place a dollop of guacamole or sour cream.
7. Sprinkle the diced onions, tomatoes (and chopped olives if you use those) around the salad.
8. Serve and enjoy! This is **REALLY** good!!!

I Can Can!! Frugal Living Series

At the request of many of her friends and family, Dr. Shambrook is currently working on a series of informative books that will guide her city friends through the domestic arts of filling a country pantry with wholesome and tasty foods on a frugal budget. No garden, compost pile, or freezer space required! The articles will show how to manage time and money and have a hearty home-cooked meal on the table in minutes by taking on a single home-canning project a couple of weekends month, based on what's on sale at the grocery store! Dr. Shambrook calls the books "quick 21st century home economics lessons for busy, frugal, health conscious working parents."

In each book, you will be guided step-by-step through the process of safely home canning a pantry staple such as beef, chicken, dried beans, or delicious relishes or salsa. The recipes are designed to be easy weekend projects for busy working-people. The books will also include recipes for preparing quick meals using the canned pantry staple so that you will be able to get nutritious and tasty food from the pantry to the table with less effort than it takes to go through the fast food drive through! Easy, well-explained, step-by-step instructions from an award winning author and home-canner will make this a manageable and satisfying project for anyone trying to fill their pantry with nutritious and flavorful food on a frugal budget.

I Can Can Beef!! How to can beef to save money and time with quick, easy, delicious family recipes (A Five Star Amazon Kindle best seller!)

I Can Can Chicken!! How to home can chicken to save money and time with quick, easy, tasty family recipes (Another Five Star Amazon Kindle best seller!)

I Can Can Relishes, Salsas & Chutneys!! (**Please do me the tremendous honor of leaving a favorable review of this book so it can have a star rating, too!**) *Available in both Kindle and Paperback formats!*

Frugal Living Series works in progress

Books slated for publication in 2013 and 2014 include:

I Can Can Ground Meats and Sausage!! (available Fall 2013)
I Can Can Turkey!! (available Fall 2013 in time for Thanksgiving turkey sales!)
I Can Can Corned Beef and Venison!! (available Fall 2013 in time for hunting season!)
I Can Can Apples!! (available Winter 2014)
I Can Can Sauerkraut!! (available Winter 2014)
I Can Can Dried Beans!! (available Winter 2014)
I Can Can Spaghetti Sauce!! (available Spring 2014)

Join one or all of the I Can Can Facebook Pages to be kept up to date when the new books become available, meet like-minded I Can Can Fans, share your canning experiences and new recipes.

About the Author

Dr. Jennifer Shambrook has a Ph.D. in Community Health Promotion and Education. She currently serves as a director at St. Jude Children's Research Hospital. She is a member of the Cherokee Tribe of Northeast Alabama. Jennifer and Robert, her husband, enjoy organic gardening, canning, travel, family time, Bible study, and Toastmasters. They keep a garden and country pantry at their home in the suburbs of Memphis, Tennessee. They have six children, with two, Sage and Daisy, still in Elementary School. The four older children (Donna, Jody, Micah and Nicole) have blessed them further with nine grandchildren and one great-granddaughter, Layla Rose.

If you have enjoyed this book, please let Jennifer know by leaving feedback on Amazon.com and drop by to say hello on the I CAN CAN Facebook pages. She had to wrestle a lot of crocodiles to get this to you!

Made in the USA
Monee, IL
16 August 2021